REVERENCE FOR LIFE

i

REVERENCE FOR LIFE

Albert Schweitzer's Spiritual
Message to Mankind

By

Walter L. Ensslin

Pioneer Publishing Company
Fresno, California
1983

Library of Congress Catalog Card Number 83-072304
ISBN 0-914330-58-6

Order additional books from:
Douglas Anderson
625 Madera Avenue, Apt. 28
Madera, California 93637

Manufactured in the United States of America
Book Publishing Center, Fresno, California

iv

TO MY FAMILY

Valeria Helene
Norbert and Monika

Mottos

In essentia unitas—in non-essentia libertas—in toto caritas. (In the essential unity—in the non-essential liberty—on the whole charity.)

What we are, is nothing—what we seek, everything. (Friedrich Hölderlin)

Great men or great causes must be served by man, lest his energies will dwindle like those of a magnet which is not laid in the direction of its poles. (Johann Wolfgang Goethe)

Always aspire to become an integrity, and if you cannot become an entity yourself, become a member of an entity. (Friedrich Schiller)

A man's reach should exceed his grasp. (Oscar Wilde)

We don't remain good if we do not always strive to become better. (Jeremias Gotthelf)

The spiritual and material misery to which mankind of today is delivering itself through its renunciation of thinking and of the ideals which spring therefrom, I picture to myself in its utmost compass. And yet I remain optimistic. (Albert Schweitzer)

Acknowledgements

Before this manuscript goes into print, I wish, nay, have to express my gratitude to the following people, without whose kind assistance and encouragement I hardly would have succeeded in completing this book:
First of all I am deeply obliged to Douglas J. Anderson, who has been not merely my typist but also an advising assistant and a stimulator, to whose inquisitive mind I owe a deeper knowledge of Carl Gustav Jung's profound and liberating psychology.
Next I owe appreciation and thanks to these individuals: Dr. Harold H. Haak, president of our university, who unreservedly encouraged my efforts to disseminate Albert Schweitzer's ethics of reverence for life; to Dr. Andrew Rippey, chairman of the Committee for Mini-Grants, and to the members thereof, Mrs. Evelyn Wright, Dr. Dallas Tueller and Dr. Russell Howland, all of whom sacrificed time and energy to evaluate the first few chapters.
Then there are two people to whom the saying applies: "The translators are the mailcoach horses of education"— namely Michael L. Stumpf and my daughter Monika.
I also owe encouragement to my wife, Valeria, who would, after reading the drafts, remark: "Das ist toll!" (that's damn good).
There are others, to be sure, to whom I must express my thanks orally or by letter, for instance Dr. Hans Margolius in Miami, Florida, "Papa Lee" Ellerbrock, etc.
As to the literature used about Albert Schweitzer, I feel the need to express my deep appreciation to Charles R. Joy for his excellent editorship of *Albert Schweitzer: An Anthology*, copyright 1947 by The Beacon Press.

Contents

Preface

There is hardly any doubt in the minds of serious philosophers of civilization that we are living in an era where all truly positive values, particularly those in the realms of philosophy, religion and ethics, are disintegrating in a heretofore unknown manner and degree. Whether we consult Oswald Spengler, Ortega y Gasset, Arnold Toynbee, Hendric de Man or others, they are, as Schweitzer is, basically pessimistic in their outlook upon our culture.

Yes, Schweitzer, too, is pessimistic about the present state of our culture and he wrote once that his thinking stands in diametrical opposition to the spirit of the age. Yet, his pessimism is a qualified one and does not encompass the entire sphere of his *Weltanschauung* (world-view). He said about himself that his knowledge (in its failure to perceive a meaningful, let alone ethical purpose in the universe) is pessimistic, but his willing and hoping are optimistic (cf. chapter five). That pessimism does, moreover, not go into great depth. It could be compared with the rippling on the surface of the stream, visible to our eye, but not reaching into the main body of the water. This one is permeated by the optimism of Schweitzer which is based upon his belief that there is much more idealism present and fermenting in mankind than we are ready to expect and to be aware of. And it is precisely this idealism which gives Schweitzer, and gives us, too, both hope and faith in the possibility of liberating mankind from the present "self-disruption of the will-to-live," from the world-wide strife and intermittent warfare, moreover, from the danger of a global disaster.

And it is this pending and terrifying danger of another world war with the catastrophic outlook of nuclear suicide and self-annihilation of so-called victors and defeated nations which urges and presses us to deeply embrace and to disseminate Albert Schweitzer's Ethics of Reverence for Life. Only this philosophy of reverence for life is able to set an end to the thoughtless fence mending in world politics and to open up an era where positive thinking will once again (as in the period of enlightenment) serve as a polar star and as a spiritual ferment to man.

With this hope in our innermost hearts we have set out to study and to disseminate Schweitzer's liberating message to mankind. May the readers or listeners open their hearts and minds to the lofty legacy of this greatest humanitarian and most devoted disciple of Jesus.

Let these words of Schweitzer conclude our preface: "The world's greatest need is spirit, because if the world is not under the rule of the spirit it will perish. Spirit is so powerful that if one could see the creation of a new spirit in the heart of humanity, all problems would be solved."

Albert Schweitzer
(An Introduction)

After Albert Schweitzer was invited in 1949 by the Institute of Humanities in Aspen, Colorado, as the principal speaker at the bicentennial celebration of Goethe's birth, America also became conscious of the greatness of this "universal" man, the jungle doctor, who had built a healing-village for the "least of us"—in response to the command of Jesus: "Follow thou me!" and his own decision on his twenty-first birthday to devote his entire life to a "direct service to mankind," as a repayment for the happiness that had been his.

Into his first thirty years he had crammed a doctorate in philosophy, another doctorate in theology (becoming the youngest-ever life-time director of his theological college of study) and had become at the same time an ordained Lutheran minister and the greatest interpreter of Bach's music through organ concerts with the Paris Bach Society, which he himself had co-founded, throughout Europe. His theological and philosophical writings and his outstanding book on Johann Sebastian Bach had already become quite famous.

When this professor then decided on his thirtieth birthday to go back to the student bench for a seven-year study of medicine—to be able to leave for Africa as a specialist on tropical diseases, dentist and psychiatrist in a self-built jungle hospital, his colleagues, family and friends thought he had "flipped his lid!"

After he had built his healing-village for the suffering and dying victims of their exploiting colonizers in the jungle (some seventy buildings), he had given to the world—at the time of his death at ninety—his personal atoning example in his plea for a *Reverence For All Life* and became an ethical beacon in our dark age. He had been called "the greatest man of our century" by the media and the electors of the Gallup Poll—and had become a legend during his own lifetime. But, as Norman Cousins once wrote, his real greatness lay in the changes he had made in the minds of his fellow men.

Throughout all this homage and the honors bestowed on him, including the Nobel Peace Prize—the money of which he used mainly for the completion of his leprosy-village—he remained a very simple and humble man. He often asked his visitors, including myself, not to write any more about him, deploring the laudatory publicity which had been showered upon him. He was sincerely grateful when I suggested that we stop only admiring him and start to think like him! He kept emphasizing that he did only a natural, simple, self-understood "thing" that we all should be doing: to hold all life, of which we are only a part, sacred with its awesome mystery—and that maintaining, enhancing and helping it in all its manifestations is our ethical, boundless responsibility.

He told me once: "An idealist must remain sober!" and so he qualified our capability of striving always for this unreachable ideal by adding: to act against this absolute ethic *never* thoughtlessly and *only* if it cannot be avoided because of a necessity forced upon us by an equally mysterious nature.

If this spiritual message of Walter Ensslin will plant the seed of "Reverence for Life" into many of our fellow men, it will have served its purpose in carrying mankind a giant step closer to a personal, ethical peace and a utopian "Peace on Earth" beyond all understanding.

Lee Ellerbrock
Conservator of the Lambarene
Hospital, 1967-1976

1. What a Man!

Is it an exaggeration to refer to Albert Schweitzer as the most outstanding humanitarian of our Western world, perhaps of all mankind? If we consider the following facts, the answer will probably be a definite affirmation of his undisputed uniqueness:

He possessed three academic degrees, two doctorates in the field of intellectual sciences—namely, one in philosophy, the other in theology—and a third one in music.

Since he was very fond of working in these fields, the study of medicine with the purpose of spending, and perhaps losing in a few years, his life as a tropical physician in Africa meant a grave sacrifice to his mind and soul.

Furthermore, in recognition of his achievements he was offered professorships by several leading universities, which would have constituted a gratifying fulfillment for his scholarly mind. Nevertheless, Schweitzer decided to decline those rewarding and honorable positions so that he might spend his entire life in that direct service to mankind of which he had already dreamed in his youth. What this decision meant to him, we can learn from his own and from other authors' writings.

Albert Schweitzer is also unique in the manner in which he saw and interpreted the personality of Jesus, and, moreover, did subject his own person and lifework in that selfless and religious devotion to a practical discipleship of Jesus. And this he did in spite of his scientifically rational and critical concept of Christ, as explained in his *Quest for the Historical Jesus*. Every glance at Schweitzer's lifework proves that to him the Gospel of Jesus was something to be lived through and acted out rather than to be merely preached and talked about.

As to the uniqueness of Albert Schweitzer, there is no doubt in my mind that one would have to dig deeply and very far back in the history of mankind in the search of an equally encompassing mind who would have taken such exacting sacrifices in a purely humanitarian service. But I doubt very much if one would ever find another humanitarian of Schweitzer's unconditional devotion and exertions in the attempt to preserve and to promote life in all of its aspects—spiritual, intellectual and physical.

2. The Decay of Our Contemporary Civilization

Albert Schweitzer had planned the publication of a Philosophy of Civilization (Kulturphilosophie) in four parts. The first part was to discuss *The Decay and the Restoration of Civilization*; the second *Civilization and Ethics*. The third part, "The World-View of Reverence for Life," did not appear as an extra book, but as chapter twenty-one of Schweitzer's work on Civilization and Ethics and is titled "The Ethic of Reverence for Life." When Schweitzer became the sole physician in a circumference of one thousand kilometers in Africa, he no longer had the time to write part four of his "Kulturphilosophie."

In the preface of his first work, Schweitzer gives this definition of civilization:

> Civilization, put quite simply, consists in our giving ourselves, as human beings, to the effort to attain the perfecting of the human race and the actualization of progress of every sort in the circumstances of humanity and of the objective world. This mental attitude, however, involves a double predisposition: first, we must be prepared to act affirmatively toward the world and life; secondly, we must become ethical.

3

For civilization to originate it is necessary that "men become inspired by a strong and clear determination to attain progress, and consecrate themselves, as a result of this determination, to the service of life and of the world. It is only in ethics that we can find the driving force for such action . . . "

We often read in Schweitzer's works that enthusiasm and self-sacrifice are the absolute prerequisites for any accomplishment of real value in the world.

In order to convince men of world- and life-affirmation and of the real value of ethics "the affirmation and ethical mentality . . . must originate in man himself as the result of an inner spiritual relation to the world." In other words, world- and life-affirmation must be the product of thought about the world and life.

Albert Schweitzer contends that with the disappearance or the obscureness of the mental disposition towards world- and life-affirmation and towards ethics we have become incapable of producing culture. Moreover, we can no longer form a correct concept of culture.

And this is the fate which has befallen us. We are bereft of any world-view. Therefore, instead of being inspired by a profound and powerful spirit of affirmation of the world and of life, we allow ourselves, both as individuals and as nations, to be driven hither and thither by a type of such affirmation which is both confused and superficial. Instead of adopting a determined ethical attitude, we exist in an atmosphere of mere ethical phrases or declare ourselves ethical skeptics.

This fatal lacking of a "Weltanschauung," a world-view, is due to the fact that our world-and-life-affirming and ethical world-view have no convincing and permanent foundation in thought. Quoting Schweitzer:

I proclaim two truths and conclude with a great interrogation. The truths are: the basic ethical character of culture, and the connection between culture and our world-view. And the question is whether a real and permanent foundation in thought can be found for a world-view which will be both ethical and affirmative of the world and of life?

If our civilization is to have a future, the meaninglessness and the hopelessness of the thoughts and convictions of modern man must be overcome.

It was as far back as February, 1923, that Schweitzer wrote that without such a general spiritual experience it will not be possible to save our world "from the ruin and distintegration towards which it is being hastened." And yet in the meantime, our suffering mankind has experienced another World War of much more terrifying dimensions in suicidal mass annihilation—including even the bestial murder by atom bombs.

Turning, in his preface, to his *Kultur und Ethik*, Schweitzer states the root-idea of his world-view:

It is that my relation to my own being and to the objective world is determined by reverence for life. This reverence for life is given as an element of my will-to-live, and becomes clearly conscious of itself as I reflect about my life and about the world. In my mental attitude of reverence for life which should characterize my contact with all forms of life, both ethics and world-and-life-affirmation are involved.

In concluding his preface, Schweitzer states that he desires above all things—and this as the crux of the whole venture— that all of us should "recognize fully that our entire lack of any Weltanschauung (world-view) is the ultimate source of all the catastrophes and misery of our times."

3. Possibilities of Recovery

Among many people there prevails the opinion that our devastating decline in culture is a result of the catastrophic world wars. Yet, the inversion of such an assessment is correct: first our mankind, particularly the Western nations, has lost the inner support and stance of culture, the result being that our spiritual vacuum was filled by the storms and debacle of reciprocal mass murder; by, in Schweitzer's words, the self-disruption of the will-to-live.

This tragedy of our spiritual chaos has been worrying not only thinkers and serious people from all strata of society, but also men and women with only modest education and in humble positions.

What can be done? sounds the question. How can our mankind recover? How can we experience a spiritual rebirth and a general therapy for our pathological societies in the world?

Most of us are lacking an answer to this solution of our gradually increasing disturbances. And many people do also master the sincerity of admitting that lack and incompetence. Others, not that sincere or pessimistic, will not admit our grave disintegration and will offer solutions which, in their final analysis, prove to be merely fence mending operations.

One of the greatest hindrances to this recovery lies in the general set-up of our entire public life, where all organizations, whether political parties, economic establishments, mass media, even scholarly and clerical institutions, are catering to the individual's membership or at least to his loyalty in thought. Most of them, especially the mass media, are exerting an influence upon the individual man and woman which is often all-powerful. Under this influence and under the stress and pressure of professional life, most people will not be able to afford the leisure and the mental collectedness to embark upon an independent and objective thinking and an analysis of the governing forces and circumstances of their lives.

There is, moreover, a widespread "self-deception as to the real conditions of our civilization" in addition to "the superficial character of modern philosophizing" and to the collapse of our previous world-view with its carrying ideals.

And yet we need not—or rather, must not—fall into a state of despair, resigning ourselves to an attitude of hopelessness in activity and a pessimistic outlook as to the possiblities of recovery. Let us emphasize the "must not," for if we assume an attitude of nostalgic resignation, then we do resemble the crew of a sinking ship that would give up any attempts to rescue the passengers and itself or, modifying the words of Schweitzer, we would act contrary to the sowman who entrusts his seeds to the soil although he does not know whether the quality of the ground or climatic conditions will ever allow the seed to germinate and to grow a plant.

All valuable activity of man evolves from and is carried by faith and we may well state that only a thoughtless fatalist will brush aside the potential blessings of faith.

4. Elemental Thinking

Albert Schweitzer always emphasizes thought and specifically elemental thinking. He believes firmly in the ability of thought to make us more inward and better—and consequently happier, too.

The paramount importance of the elemental thinking lies in the fact that it starts out from and revolves around

> ... the fundamental questions about the relations of man to the universe, about the meaning of life, and about the nature of goodness. It stands in the most immediate connection with the thinking which impulse stirs in everyone. It enters into that thinking, widening and deepening it.

We could perhaps call it common sense reflection, but one that is motivated by a serious inquisitiveness into the whither and thither of our life, in other words, about the question as to whether there is a definite meaning of life and, if so, wherein does it consist.

In his lifelong preoccupation with philosophy, Schweitzer has come to the conclusion that our contemporary philosophizing has become more and more involved in secondary issues, thus losing touch with the elemental questions about life and the world and has embarked more and more upon purely academic problems and "a mere virtuosity of philosophical technique."

And here, Schweitzer, the musician, brings one of his frequent metaphors: "Instead of genuine classical music it has frequently produced only chamber music, often excellent in its way, but not the real thing." Here, too, a comparison with our modern music, with its emphasis on technique and lack of true substance, comes to mind.

And so this philosophy, which was occupied only in elucidating itself, instead of struggling to achieve a world-view grounded in thought and essential for life, has led us into a position where we are devoid of any world-view at all, and, as an inevitable consequence of this, of any real culture.

Comparing the elemental thinking of the Greek Stoics with the simple thinking of Lao-tse and other Chinese thinkers, Schweitzer points to the importance that simple thinking is to lead man into a spiritual relation to the world and induce him to prove his unity with it by his life.

In order to facilitate the understanding of Albert Schweitzer's basic principle of ethics, Reverence For Life, we have tried to illustrate it in the diagram on page 11. We can see from it that Schweitzer did not limit his research to the Occidental philosophy alone, but included the ethics of the Oriental, too, which gave him the possibility of his complete synthesis of ethics.

Of great importance are the concepts of "elemental" and "unelemental" philosophy. Elemental he calls the thought of the Chinese, as it attacks directly the basic questions of our life, thus facilitating our search for and finding of an answer. Unelemental is the Western philosophy which soars up with its abstract windings, crowded by foreign words, into spheres so unreal and earth-removed as to remind us of our modern sky scrapers and, moreover, as to bring back from its preconceived optimistic speculations about universe, substance, thing-in-itself, Ego and Non-Ego, (World) Spirit, etc., not often so much light, but rather twilight and obstruction.

When comparing Schweitzer's applied philosophy, which "has callouses on its hands," with the soaring systems of cathedral philosophy, the superiority of the jungle doctor's spiritual edifice brings to mind that Russian fable in which the practical mind of a servant maid prevailed over the speculations of a philosopher. This one stood freezing in front of a stove, pondering how he could carry a glowing coal to his room; while the maid placed a live coal upon the dead ashes in her left hand and took it to the philosopher's stove.

It is true that the Western philosophers erected magnificent intellectual edifices, yet their painful harvest yielded no bread for the spiritually starving minds, but only gold bunions for a small stratum of speculating brain acrobats; and their value for the ethics is without adequate poise and duration, as it did not succeed, despite some good approaches, to develop a basic ethical principle of general validity. Diagram #1 also shows that both Chinese and Occidental thought are world-affirming and optimistic and at the same time ethical. This means that these thinkers departed from the unproven conception that nature and world are moral and meaningful by and in itself, i.e. ethical, and that philosophy needs only to develop a Weltanschauung which would intellectually confirm "the best of all possible worlds" (Leibniz) in an optimistic manner and to create a corresponding ethics.

In contrast to this world-and-life-affirming philosophy stands the thought of the Indians and of Schopenhauer; it is world- and life-negating and pessimistic, though also

World Philosophy

Elemental

Occidental | Chinese

Philosophy

Both world- and life-affirming

i.e. optimistic

Both ethical

Unelemental

Indian Philosophy
Schopenhauer
world- and life-
negating,
pessimistic.
Also ethical

Zarathustra
Jewish
Prophets

Active Ethics of
Self-Perfection

Passive Ethics of
Self-Perfection

SCHWEITZER'S ETHICS OF REVERENCE FOR LIFE
is the complete (i.e. passive and active) **Ethics** of
Self-Perfection.

Diagram #1

ethical. We know that the Indian is supposed with increasing age to turn away from the world and toward God, or the Nothingness (Nirvana); further, that Schopenhauer considered human life a chain of disappointments and sufferings, the only salvation of which lies in the complete resignation of the saint.

Ethics, says Schweitzer, is the activity of man directed toward the perfection of his inner personality. It can, as shown in Diagram #1, be connected with an optimistic Weltanschauung (Chinese and Occidental philosophy) or with a pessimistic one (Indian philosophy and Schopenhauer). But its scope of action is widened or contracted according to the pertinent world-view: while the optimistic Weltanschauung is developing an active ethics of self-perfecting, the pessimistic thinking leads to a passive ethics of self-perfecting and ends in resignation. Schweitzer contends quite correctly that the one and the other ethic is incomplete and therefore doomed to failure. For we are both suffering and acting beings and a complete ethics must therefore consider and influence both traits of our nature. And this is done by Schweitzer's ethics: it recognizes and encompasses both the ethics of the suffering and the acting self-perfecting.

For us civilized and educated people it is astonishing news to learn from Schweitzer and other white men that "the Negroes are deeper than we are because they don't read newspapers (words of a Caucasian to the tropical doctor). Schweitzer himself was deeply impressed by the thoughts of old natives about the ultimate things of life, about the universe, the infinite, and about our relations to each other and to mankind.

Since all valuable activity has to be grounded in thought, it is of utmost importance that thought itself should be bewinged by enthusiasm. And enthusiasm coming from thought "has the same relation to that which is produced by mere random feeling as the wind which sweeps the heights has to that which eddies about between the hills."

One of the reasons for our decline in thinking lies in the loss of common sincerity. And, indeed, if we reflect how much our modern life is permeated by a general lack of sincerity—a lack, moreover, which often is no longer felt as such—we can better understand why our great humanitarian keeps emphasizing the necessity of absolute sincerity.

Comparing our time with the era of enlightenment (rationalism), he finds it very "poor in strong men capable of loyalty to an ideal, how poor, so far as theology is concerned, in simple commonplace sincerity!" He complains about the lost feeling for sincerity. This is so much more tragical, as "sincerity is the foundation of the spiritual."

This loss of the feeling for sincerity and with it that for truth is due to our society's depreciation of thinking. How can this be helped? Only by bringing our generation again upon the road of thinking. And since Schweitzer believes that such a return is possible, he dares standing in diametrical opposition to the spirit of the age. Moreover, he takes confidently the responsibility of helping to rekindle "the fire of thought."

It is known that our Kulturphilosoph is not the only thinker who feels that "the spirit of the age dislikes what is simple," that it expects profundity from complicated elements, that it loves the violent. "The spirit of the age loves dissonance, in tones, in lines and in thought. That shows how far from thinking it is, for thinking is a harmony within us." In the same book, *Out of My Life and Thought* (if quoted again, it will be abbreviated to *Life*), Schweitzer writes these depressing words: "It will ever remain incomprehensible that our generation, which has shown itself so great by its achievements in discovery and invention, could fall so low spiritually as to give up thinking."

It gives us much to ponder that Schweitzer, himself a

devoted theologian and preacher, states in *Religion*, while dwelling on the topic of pragmatism, that our sense of sincerity is blunted "and the last thing that thinking can give humanity is a feeling for truth—for sincerity is fundamental in all spiritual life" and a shaking of this foundation entails the erosion of spiritual life itself.

One of the reasons for the lack of adequate thinking is the tragic lack of genuine freedom in our complex modern societies. Yet, unless a man is both a thinker and a free personality, he cannot comprehend culture and work for it. He must be a thinker in order to grasp and mold his ideals, says Schweitzer, and he must be free enough to disseminate his ideals into general life.

In his studies of Indian thought, Schweitzer came to realize and to formulate the two fundamental problems common to all thought: "First, the problem of world- and life-affirmation and world- and life-negation, and Second, the problem of ethics and the relations between ethics and these two forms of man's spiritual attitude to Being."

When we read Schweitzer's works, we are always astonished at how free his humanitarianism is from any dogmatic, racial, nationalistic, ideological, etc. confinements or ties. In his Gedenkrede (commemorative speech) to Goethe, we find these words of the poet:

All that thought in which a man embraces, not simply the people of a single age, but humanity itself, composed of individual human beings . . . has something superior to every age in it. Society is something temporal and ephemeral; man, however, is always man.

And a little farther down he again quotes Goethe: "Strive for true humanity! Become a man who is true to his inner nature, a man whose deed is in tune with his character."

The absolute integrity of reason and emotion, which

makes Albert Schweitzer such an extraordinary man, shows itself also in his conviction that profound thinking becomes religion. We could illustrate this marvelous unity by comparing it with a tree, branching out into two branches of equal size and power, the one representing thought, the other feeling. Needless to say that both unite not only in the root system, but already in the trunk leading thereto. Thus Schweitzer is right in his contention: "All deep religious feeling becomes thoughtful, all truly profound thinking becomes religious."

I have no doubts that some of the readers will resent Schweitzer's assertion that modern man has renounced thinking. "I have been thinking for twenty—thirty—forty, etc. years," a reader may contend, depending on his age.

And yet there is as great a difference between thinking and thinking as there is between breathing and breathing: Would a person, determined to take voice lessons, react to his teacher's introduction: "First of all you must learn how to breathe" with an exclamation of "Are you kidding? I've been breathing for twenty—thirty—forty, etc. years"? The same must-requisite of learning to breathe will be imposed upon anyone who wants to become a good swimmer.

Consequently, Schweitzer's, or any serious philosopher's admonition that we must learn to think is as sound and necessary a counsel as that of the voice and swimming teachers.

All three of them call for an *elemental* need, only that Schweitzer's call for "elemental thinking" concerns each and every single human being—so much more, indeed, as the contemporary individual—in contrast to his breathing—is being channeled and controlled by society from the cradle to the grave.

5. Optimistic and Pessimistic World-Views

As we can see in Diagram #1, both the Western and the Chinese philosophy are optimistic, that is, world- and life-affirming—whereas the Indian philosophy and Schopenhauer are pessimistic or world- and life-negating.

Albert Schweitzer maintains that an optimistic interpretation of the universe in the sense that it is ethical by and in itself, is untenable; because the universe is not only marvelously constructive, but also at the same time tragically destructive. And, as the popular saying has it: the bigger fish swallows the smaller one.

As we read in *Kultur und Ethik*, the Western philosophy has always been struggling for an optimistic outlook on life. And it is due to this prevalence of the optimistic world-view, and the permanent objection of the pessimistic philosophy of life, which enabled the peoples of Europe both in antiquity and in modern times to create culture. The question comes to mind, why our contemporary societies find themselves in such a state of fatal disintegration, despite material prosperity. Our degeneration, says Schweitzer, is due to the fact that true optimism has unnoticingly disappeared from among us. Our conception of life with all its implications has been lowered for individuals and for communities alike. "The higher forces of volition and influence are impotent in us, because the optimism from which they ought to draw their strength has become imperceptibly permeated with pessimism."

What does Schweitzer mean by true optimism? He says that it has nothing to do with over-indulgent judgments, but consists in conceiving and willing the ideal inspired by a deep and self-consistent affirmation of life and of the world. Since, however, this spirit of true optimism values all things with clear vision and impartial judgment, it appears to ordinary people as pessimism. "That it wishes to pull down the old temples in order to build them again more magnificently, is by vulgar optimism put down to its discredit as sacrilege."

The great difficulty for us in recognizing and distinguishing between optimism and pessimism lies in the fact that both inhabit the same dwelling and "go about masquerading in the clothes of the other." Thus in our present age real pessimism pretends to be optimism, and what is really optimism appears to us as pessimism.

Optimism and pessimism, being qualities not of the judgment, but of the will, "do not consist in counting with more or less confidence on a future for the existing state of things, but in what the will desires the future to be."

The characteristic faculty of a truly optimistic Weltanschauung consists in a profound world- and life-affirmation. And Schweitzer states the two things which thought has to yield to us: "It must lead us from the naive to a deepened world- and life-affirmation, and must let us go on from mere ethical impulses to an ethic which is a necessity of thought."

Can knowledge warrant an optimistic world-view to us? No. When the will-to-live begins to think, the discoveries in knowledge yield to it altogether pessimistic results. "It is not by accident that all religious world-views, except the Chinese, have a more or less pessimistic tone and bid man expect nothing from his existence here." Speaking about the constant battle going on in us between optimism and pessimism, Schweitzer illustrates it with our walking on loose stones which overhang the precipice of pessimism. When our experiences, personal or in the history of mankind, depress our will-to-live and deprive us of our freshness and conviction, we may lose our foothold and fall into the abyss together with the rock which gives way under us.

Albert Schweitzer shows the sincerity and courage to state his pessimism in judging the situation of contemporary mankind. In contrast to most of us he refuses to believe that the situation is not as bad as it appears. He is inwardly conscious that our road will lead us into "Middle Ages" of a new character. "The spiritual and material misery to which mankind of today is delivering itself through its renunciation of thinking and of the ideals which spring therefrom, I picture to myself in its utmost compass. And yet I remain optimistic." This he can afford because of his belief in truth which he preserved with certainty from his childhood. "I am confident that the spirit generated by truth is stronger than the force of circumstances." Mankind will experience the destiny which it prepares for itself by its mental and spiritual disposition. "Therefore I do not believe that it will have to tread the road to ruin right to the end."

Whereas most of us commonly speak of an optimistic and pessimistic world-view, Schweitzer sees the essential nature of a person's world-view not in his disposition to cause him to take things more or less lightly but rather in the fact of whether he has been gifted or denied the capacity of confidence: "what is decisive is his inner attitude towards Being, his affirmation or negation of life."

Schweitzer, the theologian, is well aware of the Vale of Tears which constitutes our earthly home. Dissatisfaction, disappointment and worries fill our lives. "The spiritual element in us exists in a grizzly kind of dependence on the physical." Even our very existence can be jeopardized or extinguished by meaningless events. "The will-to-live affords me an impulse to activity. But this very activity is as if I should plough the sea and sow in the furrows of it."

In view of all the setbacks or even misery to which we human beings are exposed, our will-to-live, when it begins to reflect, dashes against theories which are pessimistic through and through. That explains why all religious systems (except for the Chinese) have a pessimistic tinge. It is, moreover, not without cause and reason that many human beings put an end to their own lives. And yet there is "an instinctive impulse against such an act. The will-to-live is stronger than the pessimistic intellect. There is in us an instinctive awe in the presence of life, for we ourselves are sparks of the will-to-live."

All of us who have retained an adequate sense of observation and analysis will agree with Schweitzer that our entire notion of life has been lowered and degraded for both the individual and the masses. "The higher powers of volition and creation are becoming exhausted because the optimism from which they ought to draw their life energy has been gradually and unconsciously sapped by the pessimism which has interpenetrated its substance."

In *Civilization and Ethics* we read how pessimistic knowledge pursues us right unto our last breath.

That is why it is so profoundly important that the will-to-live should rouse itself at last, and once for all insist on its freedom from having to understand the world, and that it should show itself capable of letting itself be determined solely by that which is given within itself. Then with humility and courage it can make its way through the endless chaos of enigmas, fulfilling its mysterious destiny by making a reality of its union with the infinite will-to-live.

As we read this, two things come to our minds: a) the tragic fact that a good number of thinkers, searching for an innate meaning of the universe, ended in mental exhaustion or even collapse; and b) how much wisdom lies in these words by Goethe (who *did* have a philosophy of life): To explore the explorable and calmly to revere the unexplorable—this is the greatest gratification of the thinking man.

6. Culture, an Essentially Ethical Force

This chapter must open with an explanation of the German term "Kultur," used by Schweitzer in his writings. Although we will alternate between the words "culture" and "civilization," preference will be given to the former term—due to these reasons:

In the German philosophical disciplines, especially since Oswald Spengler (*The Decline of the West*), "Kultur" is used for the achievements and values of mind and spirit, whereas "Zivilation" encompasses the material achievements and goods of mankind's skills, technology, industrialization, etc. (The chuckle "Beethoven is culture and soap is civilization" renders the difference in a humorous way.) In the American idiom, "civilization" and "culture" are used interchangeably, but there has been a trend in recent decades to give the term culture preference when dwelling on purely intellectual, spiritual, metaphysical or, say, cultic phenomena—allegedly under the influence of German philosophy, which, like German music, has taken the lead in our Western world since aobut the eighteenth century. As to the former, Immanuel Kant (1724-1804) is the phenomenon with such an overdimensional brain (Egon Friedell, "Kulturgeschichte der Neuzeit"—*A History of Modern Civilization*), that every serious student of philosophy has to make a pilgrimage to him, just as the students of music cannot bypass the unfathomable fountain of Beethoven. Furthermore, culture renders the original content of Schweitzer's German thought vehicle with more precision; it is more metaphysical—or cultic; it is, due to its being a denominator in agriculture, horticulture, viticulture, in cultivate, easier understood by the simple man; also, it has, when pronounced, only two syllables instead of five.

Under "civilization," Mrs. Russell says that the exceptionally wide and comprehensive meaning of this word should always be kept in mind. "Dr. Schweitzer defines it as the sum-total of all progress made by mankind in every sphere of action and from every point of view, in so far as this progress is serviceable for the spiritual perfecting of the individual. Its essential element is, he says, the ethical perfecting of the individual and of the community."

In *Decay and Restoration of Civilization* we find also this brief definition of Schweitzer's: "For a quite general definition we may say that civilization is progress, material and spiritual progress, on the part of individuals as of the mass."

And in the preface, Schweitzer writes:

> Civilization, put quite simply, consists in our giving ourselves, as human beings, to the effort to attain the perfecting of the human race and the actualization of progress of every sort in the circumstances of humanity and of the objective world.

Yet this mental attitude requires a double predisposition: first, that we must act affirmatively toward the world and life and secondly, we must become ethical.

Because of the complexity of our life, it is quite important to dwell on Schweitzer's words answering his question: In what does culture consist?

First of all in a lessening of the strain imposed on individuals and on the mass by the struggle for existence. The establishment of as favorable conditions of living as possible for all is a demand which must be made partly for its own sake, partly with a view to the spiritual and moral perfecting of individuals, which is the ultimate object of civilization.

Schweitzer continues in specifying the twofold nature of culture: "It realizes itself in the supremacy of reason, first, over the forces of nature, and, secondly, over the dispositions of men."

Our modern world has achieved a remarkable progress; why should we worry so much about the decline of our culture and whether a restoration thereof is possible? The answer is that we have progressed mainly in the sphere of material goods, whereas the values of mind and spirit, or of culture, are lagging behind in a fatal discrepancy—so much, indeed, that Schweitzer considers our culture "doomed because it has developed with much greater vigor materially than it has spiritually. Its equilibrium has been destroyed."

In our intoxication about the achievements of progress we resemble children who are racing down a steep hill with their toboggan, not realizing the abyss into which they are heading.

What is essential for culture? Ethical progress is of the essence of culture and has only one significance; material progress, however, "is much less essential and may have a good or bad effect on the development of civilization."

Speaking about the manner to the restoration of culture, Schweitzer considers the ethical conception thereof as the only one that can be justified. And asking about the road that could bring us back from the horrible medley of barbarism and civilization to genuine culture, he states that the unethical conception of culture will answer: there is none.

For all symptoms of decay it sees as symptoms of old age, and culture must, like any other natural process of growth, reach its end after a certain period of time. Therefore we can do nothing, it says, but reconcile ourselves to its senility with its gradual loss of the ethical character of culture.

The ethical spirit can, however, not join in this little game of "optimism or pessimism?" Seeing the symptoms of decay as something terrible, it worries with a shudder about the future if this dying process will continue unchecked.

Thus the ethical world-view believes in a rebirth of culture, all the more so as it conceives of culture as an achievement not only of a given race, but of mankind, present and future alike. Since the urge and striving for progress has always been of utmost importance to our Western culture, Schweitzer speaks (in *Kultur und Ethik*) of three kinds of progress which come within the purview of civilization: progress in knowledge and power; progress in the social organization of mankind; progress in spirituality."

On the same page we read about the four ideals that make up for culture:

> ... the ideal of the individual; the ideal of social and political organization; the ideal of spiritual and religious social organization; the ideal of humanity as a whole. On the basis of these four ideals thought tries conclusions with progress.

The concepts of culture vary between the races of the world. So do, for instance, the Hindus not attach any importance to the material and social achievements, forming the outward and visible part of culture. (Schopenhauer espouses the same philosophy.) As a consequence of this world-view, the individual is not to trouble himself about society, nation or mankind, but must aspire merely to attain to the sovereignty of spirit over matter.

When dwelling on the ideals of true culture, Schweitzer emphasizes the ethical perfecting of the individual and of society as the essential element. Yet every spiritual and every material step in advance is significant. "The will-to-civilization is then the universal will-to-progress which is conscious of the ethical as the highest value for all."

No matter how important knowledge and extraordinary achievements are, it is nevertheless obvious that the blessings of material progress can be fully shared only by a humanity which is aspiring after ethical ends. The truth of this belief is confirmed by the negative experiences which those societies had to suffer who had confessed to an imminent progress realizing itself naturally and automatically by the dialectics of history.

The only possible way out of the present chaos is for us to adopt a world-view which will bring us once more under the control of the ideals of true civilization which are contained in it.

As to the nature of the world-view on which the universal will-to-progress and the ethical alike are founded and are linked together, Schweitzer states that it consists in an ethical affirmation of the world and of life.

In contrast to many philosophers of culture, Albert Schweitzer expresses confidence in the possibility of a restoration of our culture. He points out that the ideals of culture, needed by our age, are not new and strange to it; basically, we have nothing else to do than to restore to them the former respect and to apply them seriously in the given reality.

To the objection of historical pessimism that it is impossible to make usable and bring to power worn-out ideas, Schweitzer replies: that is true. Yet we can infer from history only what has been and not what will be. Even if no single people has ever experienced a rebirth of its decayed civilization, we have no choice but to hope and work for a reconstruction of our culture. This is possible, believes Schweitzer, if we reflect and act not from the analogy of nature, but from the laws of spiritual life.

We want to get into our hands the key of the secret, so that we may with it unlock the new age, the age in which the worn-out becomes again unworn and the spiritual and ethical can no longer get worn-out. We must study the history of civilization otherwise than as our predecessors did, or we shall be finally lost.

As we read this, our thought antenna catches the arguments of those people who believe only in facts and realities. And yet we can detect a good number of events in mankind's history which prove that, in the last analysis, it has always been a spiritual force which altered life and face of a given society. Indeed, Nietzsche was quite right: not around the inventors of new clamour does the world rotate, but around the inventors of new values. Inaudible it rotates.

Schweitzer too asserts that a spiritual element of real value influences the molding of reality so as to bring about desired results, and can thus produce facts of its own. He continues that all institutions and organizations have only a relative significance. The most diverse social and political systems have not prevented the various civilized nations to sink to the same depths of barbarism.

What we have experienced, and are still experiencing, must surely convince us that the spirit is everything and that institutions count for very little. Our institutions are a failure because the spirit of barbarism is at work in them. The best planned improvements in the organization of our society . . . cannot help us at all until we become at the same time capable of imparting a new spirit to our age.

Albert Schweitzer contends that culture is founded on some kind of world-view and that it can be restored only through a spiritual awakening and an ethical volition in mankind. These preconditions open our eyes to those difficulties in the way of a rebirth of culture which ordinary reflection would overlook. Yet it raises us simultaneously above all considerations of possibility or impossibility. If the ethical spirit yields a sufficient stance for making culture a reality, then we will get back to culture. This we can achieve by a returning to a suitable world-view by way of the convictions leading thereto.

The history of our decadence preaches the truth that when hope is dead the spirit becomes the deciding court of appeal, and this truth must in the future find in us a sublime and noble fulfillment.

We realize by now that, according to Schweitzer's philosophy, culture can only be created on the basis of an appropriate world-view, a Weltanschauung.

What exactly is meant by a Weltanschauung? Albert Schweitzer gives this answer:

It is the content of the thoughts of society and the individuals which compose it about the nature and object of the world in which they live, and the position and the destiny of mankind and of individual men within it. What significance have the society in which I live and I myself in the world? What do we want to do in the world? What do we hope to get from it? What is our duty to it? The answer given by the majority to these fundamental questions about existence decides what the spirit is in which they and their age live.

To the question what conditions a Weltanschauung must fulfill, Schweitzer gives the following answer:

First, and defined generally, it must be the product of thought. Nothing but what is born of thought and addresses itself to thought can be a spiritual power affecting the whole of mankind. Only what has been well turned over in the thought of the many, and thus recognized as truth, possesses a natural power of conviction which will work on other minds and will continue to be effective. Only where there is a constant appeal to the need of a reflective view of things are all man's spiritual capacities called into activity.

Let us conclude this chapter with one of the many pictures of Schweitzer's which remind us the age old experience that clear thinking produces also an elucidative language:

More than any other age has our own neglected to watch the thousand springs of thought; hence the drought in which we are pining. But if we only go on to remove the rubbish which conceals the water, the sands will be irrigated again, and life will spring in us where hitherto there has been only a desert.

7. The Will-to-Live

Albert Schweitzer, speaking about the will-to-live as the most immediate fact of man's consciousness, closes it in this maxim: "I am life which wills to live, in the midst of life which wills to live," and during every moment which man spends in meditating on himself and the world, he conceives himself as will-to-live surrounded by will-to-live.

As we know, the tropical doctor was, all through his life, deeply concerned about all living beings and he emphasized the fact that our ardent desire for further life and for the mysterious exaltation of the will-to-live, known as pleasure, is inherent also in the will-to-live around us; and so is the fear of destruction and of the mysterious depreciation of the will-to-live, which we call pain.

It is with remarkable psychological insight that Schweitzer pursues the functioning of the will-to-live; we begin our life in an unsophisticated world- and life-affirmation which is given to us as natural by the will-to-live that is in us. However, as we grow older and critically reflective and, moreover, attempt to reconcile knowledge and will-to-live, questions and facts crop up with confusing suggestions. We begin to experience that from the thousand attractions and expectations of life hardly one is fulfilled and that even the fulfilled expectations are almost disappointments, "for only anticipated pleasure is really pleasure; in pleasure which is fulfilled its opposite is already stirring." Unrest, disappointment and pain fill the short span of time between our birth and death. The spiritual stirrings are in a dreadful dependence on our physical nature. Our life is subject to meaningless happenings that can extinguish it at any moment. The action to which the will-to-live gives me the impulse is "just as if I wanted to plough the sea and sow in the furrows." But this does not mean that the will-to-live is bound to merge in a hopeless resignation. It does, on the contrary, also aspire to happiness and success, for as a reflective and a world- and life-affirming will-to-live it is also a will to the realizing of ideals. "But it does not live on happiness and success. . . . It sows as one who does not count on living to reap the harvest."

It is also not a flame depending on fuel provided by suitable events; it burns even with the purest light when forced to feed on its own resources. And when events seem to offer no other future but suffering, it still holds out in deep reverence for life as an active will. "Quiet and peace radiate from a being like that upon others, and cause them also to be touched by the secret that we must all, whether active or passive, preserve our freedom in order truly to live."

This means that resignation—referred to by Schweitzer as the hall leading to ethics—is not a depressing force which makes us weary of the world, "but the quiet triumph which the will-to-live celebrates at the hour of its greatest need over the circumstances of life. It flourishes only in the soil of deep world- and life-affirmation."

This triumph presupposes that will-to-live which has become thinking and has, moreover, ventured to think to the end. By doing so, it will arrive at the conclusion of Schweitzer's formula about my life as an inseparable part of all the life around me. Whoever has become reflective in this manner and scope, will no longer face his and other life in a primitive way dominated by mere instinct—nor in the confused way dominated by modern mass media and crowd-thinking, but as a free individual with his own cognition and volition, facing his and other life with reverence for life.

We remember that Schweitzer resigned to the fact that we cannot detect an ethical purpose in the universe; that our knowledge of the objective world is a knowledge from outside and must remain incomplete. But the knowledge derived from my will-to-live is direct and guides us to the mysterious movements of life itself.

Thus the highest knowledge consists in knowing that we must be true to the will-to-live. This knowledge alone hands us the compass for the journey in the night without a chart. "To live out one's life in the direction of its course, to raise it to higher power, and to ennoble it, is natural. Every depreciation of the will-to-live is an act of insincerity towards myself, or a symptom of unhealthiness."

By the same consequence, the affirmation of the will-to-live induces us to act naturally and honestly. For we confirm an act of our instinctive thought by repeating it in our conscious thought.

... The beginning of thought, a beginning which continually repeats itself, is that man does not simply accept his existence as something given, but experiences it as something unfathomably mysterious. Life-affirmation is the spiritual act in which he ceases to live unreflectively and begins to devote himself to his life with reverence, in order to raise it to its true value. To affirm life is to deepen, to make more inward, and to exalt the will-to-live.

Consequently the man who has become a thinking being feels compelled to bestow the same reverence for life to every will-to-live which he gives to his own. Experiencing that other life in his own, he will accept as being good: to preserve life and to raise it to its highest possible value; and as being evil: to destroy and injure life and to repress its development. "This is the absolute, fundamental principle of the moral, and it is a necessity of thought." ("denknotwendig" is the German term.)

This may be a repetition, but to me it seems quite necessary to stress what appears to me Schweitzer's greatest contribution to mankind—namely the discovery and proclamation of *reverence for life* as the basic principle of ethics. Although man is an egoist, he is never completely so, says Schweitzer. Our greater or smaller interest in life around us is reflected in our wishes to devote ourselves, to partake in perfecting our ideal of progress, in our desire to give meaning to life. Thus we are striving for harmony with the spiritual element.

We should not overlook the modifier "spiritual"—since we know that Schweitzer disbelieves in that will-to-harmony and perfection which philosophy and religion have repeatedly attempted to project into nature at large. We know also that the great humanitarian, despite all his respect for knowledge, maintains that it cannot give to us a satisfactory explanation about life. It can give us little, though immense information—namely this: that the will-to-live is everywhere present and that all science can lead us only to the mystery of life.

In poetical words Schweitzer describes the impulse to perfection inherent in the will-to-live: "In delicate blossoms, in the manifold wondrous forms of the jellyfish, in a blade of grass, in the crystal; everywhere it strives to reach that perfection which is implicit in its own nature."

It is superfluous to elaborate on the will-to-perfection in ourselves since it can be observed in every normal human being. Suffice it to quote Schweitzer that "we must follow if we will not be untrue to the secret will-to-live which is rooted in us."

In the face of the "horrible drama" of the world, unleashed by the tragical self-disruption (Selbstentzweiung) of the will-to-live, Schweitzer asserts that only in the thinking man the will-to-live becomes conscious of other will-to-live—and also desirous of solidarity with it. Although man cannot achieve full solidarity—since he too is subject to the horrible law of destruction and injury—he can, as an ethical being, strive to avoid the disunion of the will-to-live.

The reader will certainly enjoy this figure of speech: "The will-to-live which aspires to knowledge of the objective world is sure to make shipwreck, the will-to-live which aspires to knowledge of itself is a bold and skillful sailor."

The disruption of the will-to-live can become so vehement within man that he may reach for that tragic freedom of the will-to-live which leads him to suicide. This freedom is of particular significance for modern man who "has abundant possibilities for abandoning life, painlessly and without agony."

Yet the thinking will-to-live senses life as a mystery in which we remain by thought. "I cling to life because of my reverence for life."

Schweitzer compares the unreflective will-to-live with shipwrecked people on the waste of ocean, now enjoying an intoxicating uplift onto the crest of the wave, now despairing in their sinking moods as the ship sinks into the trough.

Thus it is with the will-to-live when it is unreflective. But is there no way out of this dilemma? Must we either drift aimlessly through lack of reflection or sink in pessimism as the result of reflection? No. We must indeed attempt the limitless ocean, but we may set our sails and steer a determined course.

All of us face the alternative of building our world-view upon a misleading knowledge of the universe or upon the direct knowledge derived from our will-to-live. And it is only the latter which can yield a solid foundation and an inner stance for our life. Our life-view is far superior to our world-view, for it is grounded in the basic principle of ethics—reverence for life.

8. Ethics, the Central Province of Philosophy

If a man from the plainland were to ask a forest dweller, "What is a forest?", the woodman's first reaction would probably be the thought: "What a silly question!"

The same thought may have come to the mind of Beethoven—to whom music was the highest possible revelation of the spirit—if one of his admirers would have posed to him the question, "What is music?" Perhaps the great composer would have burst forth with impatience: Music is spirit! Music is soul! Music is love! Music is—life pure and simple!

To the forest dweller the concept of life may be just as identical with that of the forest as to Beethoven the concept of music was one and the same as for life.

And so it was with Albert Schweitzer. His mind and soul were so intensely imbued with ethics that to him ethics was life in the truest meaning of the word; and that all his definitions and circumscriptions of the spiritual phenomenon ethics he could have spared, if it had not been for us laymen, to all of whom the question "what is ethics?" will seem just as self-evident as the two questions above.

Furthermore, to Albert Schweitzer, of whose thirty books twenty-nine were written in German, "Ethik" was not interwoven with our semantic difficulties (cf. glossary).

Yet, instead of complaining, we may rejoice about the

35

colorful garden which opens up before our intellectual eye as we look at Schweitzer's presentations on the essence and meaning of ethics.

As simple a definition as this: "Ethics is the activity of man directed to secure the inner perfection of his own personality," we find juxtaposed by this musical metaphor: "Ethics are a mysterious chord in which life-affirmation and world-affirmation are the keynote and the fifth; life-negation is the third."

In *Kultur und Ethik* we find another interesting illustration by musical means used by Schweitzer to elucidate the components in ethics: the ethics of passive self-perfecting, the ethics of active self-perfecting, and the ethics of ethical society.

Ethics thus form an extensive gamut of notes. It starts from the not yet ethical where the vibrations of resignation begin to be perceptible as notes of ethical resignation. With increasingly rapid vibrations it passes from the ethics of resignation into the ethics of active self-perfecting. Rising still higher it arrives at the notes of the ethics of society which are already becoming more or less harsh and noisy, and it dies away finally into the legal commands of society which are never more than conditionally ethical.

There is another marvelous picture which brings home Schweitzer's emphasis on the importance of mysticism.

Ethics must make up its mind to base itself in mysticism. But mysticism, on its side, must never suppose that it exists for its own sake. It is not the blossom itself, but only the green calyx which is its support. The blossom is ethics. Mysticism that exists for its own sake is the salt which has lost its savor.

We know by now that Schweitzer considers world- and life-affirmation an absolute precondition for culture. Yet without a will-to-progress which has become inward and ethical there can be only an imperfect civilization. For it is only ethics that can yield the insight to distinguish between the valuable and the less valuable, and aspire to a culture which does produce not only achievements of knowledge and power, but before all else will make both the individual and collective men more spiritual and more ethical.

In *Civilization and Ethics* we read that ethics is subjective responsibility for all life, widened out extensively and intensively to the limitless and made a reality by the man who has become inwardly free from the world experiences. This ethics originates in world- and life-affirmation and becomes a reality in qualified life-negation. "It is completely bound up with optimistic willing. Never again can the belief-in-progress get separated from ethics, like a badly-fastened wheel from a cart. The two turn inseparably on the same axle."

Ethics consist, Schweitzer says, in my experiencing the compulsion to bestow upon all will-to-live the same reverence which I do to my own. This he calls "that basic principle of the moral which is a necessity of thought" and which makes him see the good in the maintenance and encouragement of life and the bad in the destruction or obstruction of life.

After prophesying a time when people will be astonished that mankind needed so long to learn that thoughtless injury of life is incompatible with ethics, he states: "Ethics are responsibility without limit towards all that lives."

It is well known that Schweitzer's theological concepts are often quite different from those of the orthodox creeds. Yet it is perhaps less known that to him Christianity is still the best religion and that he, in contrast to millions of devoted Christians, does not only reconcile Christian faith with rationalism and profound thought, but also with the requisites of true ethics. He contends that Christianity must, clearly and definitely, decide for its members between logical religion and ethical religion and that it must insist that "the ethical is the highest type of spirituality, and that it alone is living spirituality. This will enable Christianity to reach forward to God as a living ethical spirituality. He cannot be experienced through contemplation of the world, but reveals Himself in man only"—as an ethical personality.

If the reader should feel confused about the distinction between "logical" and "ethical" religion, he may want to consider Schweitzer's attempt to come to terms with the religious thinkers of the Far East. Defining religion as the search for a solution of the problem how we can be in God and in the world at the same time, he quotes the answer given by a) Brahmanism: "By dying to the world and to life, for God is mere spirituality," and b) Hinduism: "By performing every action as something decreed by God, for God is the power which works in all."

Our theologian then argues that, by making God and the world coincide, "Hinduism blurs the difference between good and evil, which it otherwise feels with elemental vividness." The reason for this lies in that religion's desire to explain everything, to be a consistent religion emanating from logical thinking on the world.

The paramount importance of ethics as a liberating spiritual force cannot be overemphasized. It will, linked together with the universal will-to-progress and founded in a truly cultural world-view, promote the ethical perfecting of the individual and of society. Schweitzer considers such a world-view, if imbued with an ethical affirmation of life and of the world, as the only possible escape from the present chaos.

Since there has been no era in the history of mankind where the value of life itself has suffered that terrifying depreciation caused by our ruthlessly commercialized world—

dominated and disintegrated by the dreadful power of finances and machines—Albert Schweitzer's one-sentence definition: "Ethics are responsibility without limit towards all that lives" deserves our concentrated attention. As he elaborates on this brief definition, the doctor himself somewhat questions the force of its impression. Yet he still calls it the only complete ethics. For it goes far beyond compassion which is directed only to the mitigating of the suffering will-to-live; it partakes just as well in all the circumstances and aspirations of the will-to-live, its pleasure, its longing to live itself out to the full, but also its urge to self-perfecting.

It is, as always stressed by Schweitzer, thought which must determine the nature of the ethical in itself; and thinking defines it as "devotion to life inspired by reverence for life."

The universality of his ethics is once more expressed in this statement: "Ethics are reverence for the will-to-live within me and without me."

At this point we may mention Schweitzer's concept of rational or reasonable mentality and attitude. The reasonable is, and this reminds us of Hegel, also the good. And to be truly rational is to become ethical. Of course, we must not overlook the modifier "truly." It is frequently used by Schweitzer, who was well aware of the fact that the disintegration of our contemporary societies is caused mainly by the fallacy and deceptiveness of our inner values. So, he writes in his work on Indian thought that true ethics are world-wide, for all that is ethical evolves from "a single principle of morality, namely, the maintenance of life at its highest level, and the furtherance of life." To maintain our life at the highest level, we must become evermore perfect in spirit; while the highest level of other life we achieve by sympathetic and helpful self-devotion to it—"this is ethics."

Since we know by now how much Schweitzer emphasizes and reiterates sincerity, we are not surprised at this sentence: "To become ethical means to begin to think sincerely." The truth of this statement becomes quite evident when we consider to which degree our public life is permeated by misleading advertisement, by propaganda and outright lying—so much, indeed, that one can assume that the world would finally experience a cessation of hatred, strife and warfare if mankind would succeed in recognizing and outlawing the lie in itself as the cardinal sin to be abhorred and exterminated before and above all other malice.

9. The Search for the Basic Principle of Ethics

In his search for the "basic" or "fundamental principle of the moral" (or ethics) Schweitzer goes back to the Greek and Roman philosophers. Above and beyond that he also investigates the ethics of the Chinese and the Indian thinkers, for instance Lao-tse, Chwang-tse, Lie-tse; further the Indian Brahmans, also Buddha and the Oriental philosophers in general.

Schweitzer maintains that "the basic principle of the moral must be recognized as a necessity of thought (denknotwendig), and must bring men to an unceasing, living, and practical conflict and understanding with reality."

As to the principles of the moral which had hitherto been developed, they are "absolutely unsatisfying." For if we attempt to think them out to a conclusion, they will either lead to paradoxes, or will lose in ethical content.

The classical thinkers tried to conceive of the ethical as that which brings rational pleasure. But this point of departure did not lead to an ethic of active devotion. "Confined to the egoistic—utilitarian, it ended in an ethically-colored resignation."

The ethical thought of modern times, which is from the outset social-utilitarian, demands as a matter of course that the individual must devote himself in every respect to his neighbors and to society. But in its attempts to give a firm foundation to the ethic of altruism, considered so much a matter of course, it fails to think that matter out to a conclusion and arrives at the most remarkable consequences which are inconsistent with each other in the most varied directions.

After elaborating in more detail on these inconsistencies, Schweitzer states that the ethic of altruism, being always in too much of a hurry to reach practical results, ends by selling its soul to biology and social sciences, "which lead it to conceive itself as herd-mentality, wonderfully developed and capable of still further development. And with this it finally sinks far below the level of real ethics."

Although the basic principle of ethics seemed to be within the reach, "the ethics of altruism always grasped to right or left of it."

Consequently the ethic of altruism cannot develop into a system which satisfies thought.

Besides these two attempts to conceive of ethics either as a means to gain rational pleasure, or as devotion to the fellow-individuals and to society, there is a third system, which explains ethics as effort for self-perfecting.

Schweitzer asserts that this enterprise is somewhat abstract and venturesome. Being reticent to start from a generally accepted content of the ethical, as utilitarianism does, it expects thought to derive the entire content of ethics from the effort for self-perfecting.

Plato and Schopenhauer, these two Occidental adherents to the ethics of self-perfecting, espoused, as do the Indians, world- and life-negation as the basic principle of the ethical. Yet world- and life-negation does, if consistently thought out and developed, not produce ethics but reduces it to impotence—says Schweitzer.

Immanuel Kant, this veritable giant among the modern philosophers (1724-1804) restored the ethics of self-perfecting, introducing the conception of absolute duty. But he does not imbue it with a specifically defined content. In his mind, one should surmise, the content was self-evident as that good which Lincoln must have had in mind when he said: "When I do good, I feel good. When I do bad, I feel bad. This is my religion."

Yet Schweitzer denies Kant the ability "to derive the content of ethics from the effort for self-perfecting."

In chapter nine of his *Kultur und Ethick* Schweitzer gorical Imperative, but preferred in his *Metaphysik der Sitten* (A Metaphysics of Morals, 1797) to assign to ethics perfection. His Categorical Imperative—"Act in such a way that you use human nature both in your own person and in everyone else's always as an end, never merely as a means"— consituties a satisfactory principle of ethics for the great philosopher as well as for any individual susceptible for moral postulates—whether these be expressed in words or in the sounds of great composers, the paintings of great painters or the sky-soaring steeples of great cathedrals. But the great majority of men can hardly be moved to really moral conduct unless the ethical principles are spelled out to them in such an articulate exposure that their minds and hearts can open up to them as bud and blossom open up to the sunlight.

As to Kant's ethical searching, Schweitzer objects that he did not develop the totality of ethical duties out of his Categorical Imperative, but preferred in his "Metaphysik der Sitten" (A Metaphysics of Morals, 1797) to assign to ethics two goals, the perfecting of oneself and the happiness of others and to elaborate upon the virtues which promote them.

Is Schweitzer right in his criticism of the great philosopher? The answer can only be "yes" if we consider the following requisites of true ethics:

First, the concept of duty, regardless of how deep the devotion of a person will be, need not be ethical by and in itself.

If it were so, then all the glorification and honors bestowed upon the most successful warriors would mean that injury and extermination of human and other life were a moral venture. (Yet, as we know, even the lives of coyotes and rattlesnakes are spared where the balance of ecology calls for it.)

Secondly, a basic principle of ethics must—if human beings consider the existence and survival of mankind not only a worthwhile theory, but a bare necessity of the cosmic order, meaning, and harmony—espouse and clearly articulate the preservation and promotion of life. Moreover, not only its procreation but its elevation.

Thirdly, a fundamental principle of the moral must be so universal or all-inclusive that all life is sheltered and protected by its spiritual radiation.

Kant's ethics, however, although concerned with the prohibition of cruelty to animals, limits the boundaries of his ethical postulates to the duties of man to man—ignoring the relations of man to non-human existence.

There is, of course, no doubt that Kant's ethics is also founded and grounded in thought—as were all his magnificent works. But his categorical imperative of duty, no matter how loftily conceived and how brilliantly advocated, remains without effect among all those human beings whose primitive cultures simply do not possess that sense of duty and responsibility which has developed as an outgrowth of civilizations counting their age by centuries. On the other hand, Schweitzer's basic principle of "reverence for life" and, moreover, his insistence upon the sacredness of all life can easily be understood by even the most underdeveloped tribes; for it emerges as naturally out of the will-to-live as a plant grows out of the soil.

If a person wanted to defend Kant's implied benevolence in duty, he could argue that Schweitzer's assertion about thinking being a harmony within us is also lacking specified modifiers, such as constructive or positive or life-centered, life-preserving, life-promoting, or meaningful, etc. think-ing. Yet we know beyond doubt that the doctor's concept of thinking definitely implies such modifiers.

As a side remark, we should point to the inestimable value of any principle which is born out of thought—be it that of Schweitzer or any other thinker—namely the fact that it will be free from fanaticism. Because fanaticism has its roots and gains momentum in emotions, and as soon as there is no adequate power of thought or reason to act as a filter and counterpoise for emotions, fanaticism will overwhelm all judicious reflection.

As to the boundaries of ethics, Schweitzer is quite right to contend that by limiting the sphere of the ethical to the relations of man to man would preempt all attempts to reach a basic principle of ethics with an absolutely binding content.

Schweitzer argues that Kant passes by the problem of finding a basic ethical principle with a definite content because he pursues an object which lies outside ethics. He wants to combine ethical idealism with an idealistic world-view based upon a theory of knowledge. "From that source he hopes there will come an ethical philosophy capable of satisfying critical thought."

In chapter nineteen of his "Kultur und Ethik" Schweitzer maintains that ethics has nothing to expect from any theory of knowledge. To depreciate the reality of the material world brings apparent profit only. An ethical interpretation of the world could yield real ethics as little as world- and life-affir-mation could be gained from an optimistic interpretation of it. Ethics must rather find their foundation in themselves in an absolutely mysterious world.

Schweitzer says that so far all ethical systems have re-mained quite fragmentary and that they confined themselves to this or that octave of the gamut. While the Indians, and Schopenhauer, were only concerned with the ethic of passive self-perfecting, Zarathustra, the Jewish prophets, and the great moralists of China adhered to that of active self-perfecting. Modern Western philosophy busied itself mostly with the ethic of society. The European thinkers of antiquity cannot get beyond the ethic of resignation. "The deeper thinkers among our moderns—Kant, J. G. Fichte, Nietzsche, and others—have inklings of an ethic of active self-perfecting."

European thought is mostly playing in the upper octaves, says Schweitzer, and not in the lower ones. "Its ethic has no base because the ethic of resignation plays no part in it. An ethic of duty, that is to say, an activist ethic, appears to it to be complete."

To Schweitzer the fatal weakness of modern European thought is its inability to understand resignation and the relations between ethics and resignation.

A complete code of ethics consists, according to the tropical doctor, in "ethics of passive self-perfecting, combined with ethics of active self-perfecting."

In his exacting search for the basic principle of ethics Schweitzer went through a painful experience, reminding us of the tedious process of a plant feeling its way from the dark soil into daylight. After he had tormented his mind as if running against an insurmountable wall, the phrase "reverence for life" struck him like a sudden flash of light out of the darkness.

What is this basic principle of the moral?

Our great humanitarian says:

The basic principle of ethics, that principle which is a necessity of thought, which has a definite content, which is engaged in constant, living, and practical dispute with reality, is: Devotion to life resulting from reverence for life.

10. Individual Ethics and Social Ethics

An anecdote from ancient Greece tells us of an orator who, when the crowd broke out into applause, turned to his friend with the question, "Have I said anything wrong?"

Whether this really happened or not is quite immaterial. Important is the hidden truth that there was an era when the individual was aware of the fact that even the most judicious man, when he becomes a link or a kernel in a crowd, may lose his independent thinking.

It is of course needless to state that Schweitzer is not the only thinker who voices his concern and warning about the loss of the individual's worth and value.

We find, for instance, in Carl Gustav Jung's works almost literal parallels in his analyses of the individual's intellectual and spiritual captivity within modern society. In his book, *The Undiscovered Self*, he writes that even the churches strive at "mass action in order to cast out the devil with Beelzebub—the very churches whose care is the salvation of the individual soul." And further down (on page 68): "It is, unfortunately, only too clear that if the individual is not truly regenerated in spirit, society cannot be either, for society is the sum total of individuals in need of redemption."

Jung's statement that it is time for us to ask "exactly what we are lumping together in mass organizations and what

47

constitutes the nature of the individual human being, i.e., of the real man and not the statistical man" could just as well be a sentence from a Schweitzer text.

It is quite tragical, indeed, that we lost the medieval view of man as a microcosmos, "a reflection of the great cosmos in miniature," of which the great psychiatrist speaks. Exactly as Schweitzer, so does Jung consider the individual personality "as the only direct and concrete carrier of life" and society and the State as conventional ideas, the reality of which depends on a certain number of individuals. Again the reader of Jung's passage below will immediately recall those nearly identical warnings of Schweitzer.

With credulity come propaganda and advertising to dupe the citizen with political jobbery and compromises, and the lie reaches proportions never known before in the history of the world.

These ideas from the book mentioned above find reflectons and confirmation in other works by C. G. Jung, for instance in his *Modern Man in Search of a Soul.*

Very similar words we hear for example from Margaret Mead—to mention one of the great modern anthropologists.

Elaborating on the problem of the renewal of civilization, Schweitzer contends that it has nothing to do with movements reflecting the experiences of the crowd—which are nothing but reactions to external happenings. Yet a revival of culture is possible only when a new tone of mind will arise, a tone of mind independent of and in opposition to the mentality of the crowd, a tone of mind which will gradually prevail over the collective one, determining in the end its character. "It is only an ethical movement which can rescue us from the slough of barbarism, and the ethical comes into existence only in individuals."

As long as our reliance upon facts and, linked with it, our

reliance on organizations does prevail, we will not succeed in perfecting or reforming our public and social life and must therefore fail in that progress which alone could restore our disintegrating culture.

Schweitzer maintains that of all the forces which mold reality, morality is the first and foremost. This being the case, everyone who believes that he can help forward the ethical will-awareness of individuals and of society has the right to speak now, says Schweitzer, regardless of the fact that political and economic questions are put on top of the present day agenda. Lasting accomplishments in political and economic life can be gained only if we approach them by ethical thinking.

The collapse of our culture has occurred "because we left the whole question of ethics to society." An ethical revival will only set in when ethics again becomes the concern of thinking men and when individuals begin to asset themselves in the community as ethical personalities. Only by this process can society be transformed from a purely natural body into an ethical organism.

Such a transformation is absolutely necessary, since the ethical perfecting of individuals and of society is the essential element in culture.

To which dreadful extent the individual personality has become a prisoner of society is clearly reflected by the fact that human creatures are actually being numbered—not only in jails, but also in public institutions of all kinds. This degrading of the individual has experienced its utmost completion in the Soviet Union, presenting itself externally already in the private sphere of letters, the addresses of which bear the omnipotent State on top and the name of the individual as the last item on the very bottom.

Schweitzer, speaking about our rich inheritance from the past, says that it has been squandered; and that we are sinking today into a state of spiritual and intellectual poverty. I wrote several decades ago that modern man was renouncing inalienable rights of the individual—and that this made our race incapable of producing new ideals or of making current ones serviceable for new objects. Modern man's only experience in this field is that prevailing ideas obtain more and more authority, take on a more and more one-sided development, and live on till they have produced their last and most dangerous consequences.

It is known to everyone how authoritarianism is being criticized in those countries where the governments are nothing but an alleged elite of the single political party in existence. Yet it is also true what Schweitzer asserts, namely our need for a "society, a faith and a church that respect and exalt the individual, calling forth all the powers of ethical thought and devotion that are innate within him." Most churches are liable to have dogmatism prevail over unhampered thinking in the pursuit of truth. The theologian Schweitzer deplores the disappearance of liberal piety due to the fact that most of the Christian legacy is creedal and dogmatic. Even in the universities "the liberal spirit is being extinguished."

In the face of this hazardous predominance of mass thinking over individual thought, of the "Zeitgeist" or public opinion over private opinion, our boasting with the freedom and dignity of the individual becomes well-nigh ridiculous.

Of course, in our American democracy there is indeed a good deal of personal liberty, which may be used by the law abiding citizen in a beneficial way and which is being used by any unlawful character not as mere liberty but as sheer license. These external phenomena do not, to be sure, mean that the Western societies and indeed all societies of the present era, do possess and offer a philosophical system, a

Weltanschauung, which could function like a parachute, protecting both individuals and nations from falling into the abyss of spiritual nihilism and chaos.

As a matter of fact, the present state of our spiritual climate is liable to evoke the diagnosis that in our psychic disturbed societies only he is normal who is no longer "quite normal."

This perhaps somewhat cynical intermezzo finds more than adequate support with, I believe, all serious philosophers, psychologists, sociologists, and last but not least, with the humanitarian thinker Albert Schweitzer.

Already in *The Decay and the Restoration of Civilization* he writes that it is perhaps the most characteristic trait in modern man that he is lost in the mass to a degree without precedent in history. His diminished concern about his inner nature makes him susceptible to the views of society and its mass media to an almost pathological extent. Since, moreover, our well-organized societies have become a heretofore unknown power in the spiritual life, man's lack of independence makes him almost renounce a spiritual existence of his own. Like a rubber ball which has lots its elasticity and preserves indefinitely every impression under the thumb of the mass, he draws from it all his opinions, be they national or political or those of his own belief or unbelief.

As a great admirer or even disciple of Johann Wolfgang Goethe, Schweitzer lectured and wrote about this giant of universal mental and spiritual ingenuity. He stresses, of course, Goethe's views on the dignity and value of the individual personality and of individual thought. Thus Goethe contends that all that thought in which humanity itself, as a sum total of human beings, is embraced, is superior to every age in it. "Society is something temporal and ephemeral; man, however, is always man," says Goethe.

Schweitzer also mentions that Goethe's message to the men of today is the same as to the men of his time and of all times: "Strive for true humanity! Become a man who is true to his inner nature, a man whose deed is in tune with his character."

Goethe does also admonish the individual not to abandon the ideal of personality, even when it contradicts the developing circumstances; and not to give it up for lost even when it seems untenable amidst opportunistic theories which demand that the spiritual confirm to the material.

"Remain men in possession of your own souls! Do not become human things which have given entrance to a soul which conforms to the will of the masses and beats in time with it." (Goethe)

In *Kultur und Ethick* (chapter nineteen) Schweitzer explains why the ethic of ethical personality cannot succeed in developing into a serviceable ethic of society; although it seems so obvious, that from right individual ethics right social ethics should result; and that the system of the former should continue into the latter like a town into its suburbs. Yet, in reality they cannot be built so that the streets of the one extend into those of the other. "The plans of each are drawn on principles which take no account of that." Here are the reasons for this tragic dilemma:

> The ethic of ethical personality is personal, incapable of regulation, and absolute; the system established by society for its prosperous existence is supra-personal, regulated, and relative. Hence the ethical personality cannot surrender to it, but lives always in continuous conflict with it, obliged again and again to oppose it because it finds its focus too short.

Schweitzer says that, in the last resort, the antagonism between the two is rooted in their differing valuations of humaneness. Humaneness consists in the principle that a human being is never to be sacrificed to a purpose.

Now, whereas the ethic of ethical personality aims at preserving humaneness, "the system established by society is impotent in that respect."

Schweitzer elaborates on the ability of the individual to bear a loss himself when being faced by the alternative to sacrifice the well-being or the existence of another person while society, thinking and proceeding supra-personally, cannot attribute the same weight to individual well-being or existence.

It goes without saying that a supra-personal ethic is in principle non-humanitarian.

Any society, in order to reach its goals, will always be tempted to limit the authority of individual ethics, although it must inwardly acknowledge its superiority. But it needs servants who will never oppose it.

One of the most deceptive and perilous attributes of social organizations is the magical belief in numbers. They constantly befool us and themselves with such shallow slogans as: twenty million citizens—or men, women, trade unionists, etc.—can't be wrong.

Since slogans allegedly are bullet-proof against counterarguments, we must consider ourselves lucky when a witty mind disarms them with their own weapon—for example, "five thousand coyotes can't be wrong," a chuckle in praise of Colorado.

The picturesque language of the universalist Schweitzer delights and spurs our imagination by his marvelous intertwining of philosophy, religion, psychology, sociology and, last not least, music. As he elucidates how individual struggles for humanity can become powerful amidst the present mentality, he shows how we can serve society without abandoning ourselves to it; and without allowing it to be our guardian in the matter of ethics. "That would be as if the solo violinist allowed his bowing to be regulated by that of the double-bass player." Our mistrust of the ideals established by society we will never lay aside, realizing that "society is full of folly and will deceive us in the matter of humanity. It is an unrealiable horse, and blind into the bargain. Woe to the driver, if he falls asleep!" Already in *Verfall und Wiederaufbau der Kultur (Decay and Restoration . . .)* Schweitzer writes that the demoralization of the individual by the mass is in full swing.

The man of today pursues his dark journey in a time of darkness, as one who has no freedom, no mental collectedness, no all-round development, as one who loses himself in an atmosphere of inhumanity, who surrenders his spiritual independence and his moral judgement to the organized society in which he lives, and who finds himself in every direction up against hindrances to the temper of true civilization. Of the dangerous position in which he is placed philosophy has no understanding, and therefore makes no attempt to help him. She does not even urge him to reflection on what is happening to himself.

The terrible truth that with the progress of history and the economic development of the world it is becoming not easier, but harder, to develop true civilization, has never found utterance.

11. The Ethic of Self-Perfecting and the Ethic of Self-Devotion

The Russian writer Anton Čexov relates in his short story "The Bet" how a young lawyer confines himself voluntarily to fifteen years of seclusion, at the end of which period a rich banker will pay him two million rubles.

If we may surmise that the lawyer fancied the years would not be too much of an ordeal when spent in a consistent pursuit of self-perfecting studies, then we could draw two conclusions in order to explain the fact that the young m;an not only turned into a veritable skeleton, but also voluntarily broke the contract by escaping from his confinement five hours before the agreed deadline—these conclusions being:

First, a process of self-perfecting (whether for two million rubles or for the sake of self-perfecting as such) must lead to an unconditional negation of the world and of life (the prisoner explicitly stated his unconditional and absolute contempt of everything men and the world can offer);

Secondly, a human being cannot survive in a hermetic and meaningless isolation from his fellow men—a fact finding its elucidation in Schweitzer's repeated statements that no man lives for himself alone but always together with and for his fellow men.

Needless to say that a pursuit of knowledge or art merely

for the sake of those disciplines cannot yield meaning and content to life. And thus Nietzsche is quite right with his postulate: we want to serve knowledge only so far as knowledge is serving life.

In *Kultur und Ethik* Schweitzer contends that, although ethics must originate in mysticism, the hitherto accepted mysticism, being abstract, leads into the supra-ethical. Yet abstraction is the death of ethics, he says, for ethics are a living relationship to actual life.

This reminds us of the modern abstractions in the arts, be it architecture, painting or music, all of which reflect the appalling decay of our civilization. In this context I recollect that Ortega y Gasset, too, spoke about the "taboo" which the modern artist has imposed on the truly humane or aesthetic values.*

The history of philosophy had coined words to express man's conception of the infinite creative force by designations like the Absolute, the Spirit of the Universe, the Essence of Being, the Substance, and similar terms. Now, it may surprise those readers who know Schweitzer as a unique idealist that he refutes such expressions as denoting nothing actual, but something conceived in abstractions and therefore absolutely unimaginable. "The only reality is the Being which manifests itself in phenomena."

Schweitzer answers his own question about how thought came to such a meaningless proceeding—as making man enter into a spiritual relation with an unreal creation of thought—by explaining the yielding to a double temptation, one general, one particular.

The general consists in thought, compelled to express itself in words, adopting the abstractions and symbols coined by language as its own abstractions. Although this

*In *The Dehumanization of the Arts* (or in *The Revolt of the Masses.*)

coinage should have no more currency than that limited by the need to represent things in an abbreviated way, in time thought ends up by using these abstractions and symbols as if they represented something which really exists.

Nomina sunt Realia (names are realities) was the medieval formula expressing what Schweitzer calls the general temptation.

The particular temptation lies in the enticingly simple way in which man's devotion to infinite Being is expressed with the help of abstractions and symbols. This way is meant to consist of entrance into relation with the totality of Being, that is with its spiritual essence.

Schweitzer maintains that this looks very good in words and thoughts, but that reality knows nothing of a possibility for the individual being to enter into connection with the totality of Being. The only Being of which it knows is that which manifests itself in the life of individual beings, and consequently the only relation known to it is the relation of one individual being to another.

By the same consequence mysticism, to be honest, can do nothing but abjure the usual abstractions and admit that it can do nothing rational with this imaginary Essence of Being. "The Absolute may be as meaningless to it as his fetish is to a converted Negro." It must in all seriousness go through the conversion to the mysticism of reality. "Abandoning all stage decorations and declamation, let it try to get its experience in living nature."

Schweitzer sees "no Essence of Being, but only infinite Being in infinite manifestations." Thus, my being can have any intercourse with infinite Being only through those relations which I enter with the manifestations of Being. And my devotion to infinite Being means devotion of my being to all the manifestations of Being in need of and susceptible to my devotion.

Since only an infinitely small part of infinite Being comes

within our range, the rest passes us by like distant ships which do not understand our signals. But by devoting ourselves to all the life within our sphere and need of influence, we "make spiritual, inward devotion to infinite Being a reality"; and, by so doing, we give our own poor existence meaning and richness, says Schweitzer. "The river has found its sea."

In his search for a complete ethics, Schweitzer analyzes and grapples with both the ethic of self-perfecting and the ethic of self-devotion.

He admits that the ethic of self-perfecting is fundamentally cosmic—yet it must, if it is to combine with the ethic of self-devotion, first become cosmic in the right way.

It is fundamentally cosmic, since self-perfecting consists of man coming into his true relationship with the Being both within him and outside him. Man strives to change his natural, outward connection with Being into a spiritual, inward devotion, "letting his passive and active relation to things be determined by his devotion."

Yet in this effort he has never advanced beyond a passive self-dedication to being. As to active self-dedication, he is always driven past it.

Someone may argue that the ethic of self-perfecting needs not be universal by its nature, that it can be quite self-centered, even to the point that it gives not a penny to society and its demands. This may be especially eclatant with artists, since "a talent is built up in the stillness" (Goethe). Nevertheless, even if art for the sake of art has as little ethical content as science for the sake of science would have, we do not mean to say that an artist, aiming at veritable self-perfection, would not be imbued by that feeling of cosmic oneness with the infinite Being which constitutes part and parcel of every type of profound art, particularly with the great forms of music.

In his comparative studies of the European and Oriental

religious and philosophical systems, Schweitzer comes to
the conclusion that the battle of Brahmanism and Buddhism
with Christianity is a battle between the spiritual and the
ethical. He quotes Indian defenders of their philosophy as
maintaining that "spirituality is not morality—that is, to
become spiritual by merging into the divine is something
apart, something which ultimately, being supreme, is above
all ethic." We Christians, however, assert: "Spirituality and
morality are one and the same. It is through the most thoroughgoing morality that the highest spirituality is attained,
through the most thoroughgoing morality that it is continually expressed."

In spite of all due credit to the Eastern theories, such as
their impressive unification in itself, the logical consistency
and the profound value in leading men to introspective
thinking about themselves and their relation to Being,
Schweitzer nevertheless considers them a "poverty-stricken
religion." For its God is mere empty spirituality, its last
word to us is absolute negation of life and world and its
ethical content is meager. "It is a mysticism which makes
man lose his individual existence in a god that is dead."

As to the ethical content of Christian mysticism Schweitzer
mentions that it also is alarmingly small.

Expressing himself in a metaphor, while comparing the
Indian and the Christian ideas of the divine, the doctor calls
the former a pure spiritual essence and an ocean into which
man, tired of swimming, wishes to sink; while the God of
Jesus is living ethical Will, leading my will into a new direction and urging me: "Strike our courageously! Do not ask
where your efforts will take you on the infinite ocean. It is
my will that you should swim."

The Indian thinkers are not unaware of the shortcomings
within their mentality: at times Vivekananda expresses his
despair that the West has attained to great social achievements, while in India, the home of eternal verities, the poor

and the suffering are grossly neglected. Here are two sentences by Vivekananda: "No society puts its foot on the neck of the wretched so mercilessly as does that of India. . . . So far as the spiritual and mental qualities are concerned, the Americans are greatly our inferiors, but as a social community they are superior to us."

According to Schweitzer three components go into ethics: the ethic of passive self-perfecting, which is resignation achieved by inward self-liberation from the world; the ethic of active self-perfecting, effected through mutual relations between human beings; and the ethic of ethical society. (Here the reader may want to take a look at the diagram on page 11.)

We had mentioned that man's innate longing for self-perfection urges him to change his natural, outward connection with being into a spiritual, inward devotion, a devotion which determines his passive and active relation to things.

Yet his efforts have so far not been able to carry him beyond a passive self-dedication to being.

The reason that the ethic of self-perfecting could not break through the circle of the passive lies in the fact that its spiritual inward devotion to being has been directed to an abstract totality of being instead of to real being. "So nature-philosophy is approached in a wrong way."

Be it mentioned here in all brevity that Schweitzer, in his attempt to come to grips with the problem of the confinement and the following ineffectiveness of the ethic of passive self-perfecting, discusses the Chinese efforts to comprehend the ethic of self-perfecting within nature-philosophy.

Yet this cannot lead out of the dilemma. Because there are no motives of ethical activity to be discovered in nature, and therefore "the ethic of self-perfecting must allow both active and passive ethics to originate side by side in the bare fact of spiritual inward self-dedication to being." Schweitzer contends that both must be derived from action as such, without presupposing any moral quality in being. Only in this way thought will reach a complete system of ethics without becoming "guilty of any sort of naive or tricky proceedings." In contrast to the Oriental thinkers, the Western mentality does not open the doors to mysticism, because it feels by instinct that it opposes activist ethics, and consequently there is no inward relationship to it.

But it is our great mistake, says Schweitzer, to assume that an ethical world- and life-view, which would satisfy thought, can be reached without mysticism. So far we have done nothing but compose world- and life-views. They are good in so far as they keep us up to activist ethics, but they are not true and therefore do always collapse. They are, moreover, shallow.

Hence European thought makes men ethical indeed, but superficial, and the European, because he is surfeited with philosophy which has been fabricated with a view to activist ethics, has no equanimity and no inward personality, nor indeed any longer a feeling of need for these qualities.

Toward the end of his book on the decay and restoration of culture Schweitzer dwells on the Westerner's dream of a Weltanschauung which corresponds to our impulse to action, clarifying it at the same time. We have not succeeded in a definite formulation of such a world-view, and thus we possess merely an impulse without any definite orientation. "The spirit of the age drives us into action without allowing us to attain any clear view of the objective world and of life." By claiming our inexorable toil for this or that end or achievement, it keeps us in an intoxication of activity ["workaholic" is an illustrative cue] depriving us of any time needed to reflect and to pose the question about whether there is any meaning of the world and of our lives in this restless sacrificing to ends and achievements.

And so we wander hither and thither in the gathering dusk formed by lack of any definite theory of the universe like homeless, drunken mercenaries, and enlist indifferently in the service of the common and the great without distinguishing between them. And the more hopeless becomes the condition of the world in which this adventurous impulse to action and progress ranges to and fro, the more bewildered becomes our whole conception of things and the more purposeless and irrational the doings of those who have enlisted under the banner of such an impulse.

We have gathered by now that the ethic of self-perfecting and the ethic of self-devotion have lived side by side and without finding a means to combine their ideas into a true basic principle of the moral.

Schweitzer, posing the question why they do not succeed in mutual interpenetration of thought, gives the following explanation:

The fault with the ethic of self-devotion must be sought in the fact that it is too narrow. Because social utilitarianism is, by its principle, only concerned with the self-devotion of man to man and to human society; whilst the ethic of self-perfecting, being universal all right, confines itself within the relation of man to the world. Now, in order that these two systems of ethics come into agreement with each other the ethic of self-devotion must become universal, too, and must direct its devotion not merely towards man and society but also towards all life in the world.

Yet until now ethics have not taken even the first step toward a universalizing of altruism.

Just as the housewife who has scrubbed out the parlor takes care that the door is kept shut so that the dog may not get in and spoil the work she has done by the marks of his paws, so do European thinkers watch carefully that no animals run about in the fields of their ethics.

Schweitzer continues by pointing out the fact that the stupidities of which they are guilty in maintaining the traditional narrow-mindedness border on the incredible. If they do not leave out altogether all sympathy for animals, they take care that it shrinks to a mere afterthought without any meaning. And if they admit more than that, they feel obliged to bring elaborate justifications or even excuses.

"It seems as if Descartes with his dictum that animals are mere machines had bewitched the whole of European philosophy."

In contrast to the European thinkers, such as Wilhelm Wundt,* Bentham, Darwin (exceptions to these are Schopenhauer, Stern, and others), the Chinese and Indian ethics command a kindly relation to all creatures—having, moreover, attained to this attitude "quite independently of each other."

The reason why the European philosophy refused to make self-devotion universal, lies in its efforts to reach a rational morality containing universally valid judgments, which it deems possible only upon the solid ground of the interests of human society. It also wants to conceive of ethics as a well-ordered system of duties and commandments which can be well fulfilled.

---

*"To crown this wisdom [that man is the only object for sympathy ... CE.239] he ends with the assertion that of rejoicing with animals there can at any rate be no question, as if he had never seen a thirsty ox enjoying a drink."

Yet Schweitzer maintains that the principle of love, even if limited to human beings, will lead us to an ethic of boundless responsibilities and duties. Consequently the solid ground sought by philosophy must be abandoned as soon as we begin to discuss existence as such. "Willing or unwilling, ethics have to plunge into the adventure of trying to come to terms with nature-philosophy, and the outcome cannot be foreseen." Not only is this a correct conclusion, says Schweitzer, but, as has already been shown, the standard morality of society (if it can be formulated as a system at all) does never yield a true code of ethics but only an appendix thereto. True ethics are, we must repeat, always subjective and are, moreover, propelled by an irrational enthusiasm; they must, furthermore, be in conflict with nature-philosophy. Consequently, the ethic of altruism has no reason to dodge this unavoidable adventure. "Its house has been burnt down. It can go out into the world to seek its fortune."

In conclusion we should again stress the truth that ethics must embrace the thought that self-devotion has to be directed not only towards man but towards all living beings, indeed, towards all life whatever in the world. Ethics must rise to the conception that the relation of man to man is nothing but an expression of that relation in which we all stand to being and to the world in general. "Having thus become cosmic, the ethic of self-devotion can hope to meet the ethic of self-perfecting, which is fundamentally cosmic, and unite with it."

12. Schweitzer's Complete Ethics of Reverence for Life

Schweitzer writes that every world- and life-view which is to satisfy thought is mysticism. It must seek to give to our existence such a meaning that we will not be satisfied with being a part of the infinite existence merely by nature, but will spur our determination to belong to it in soul and spirit as well, through an act of our consciousness.

Now, as to the ethic of self-perfecting, it stands in inmost connection with mysticism. But mysticism itself is only in so far a valuable world- and life-view as it is ethical.

Yet, as we remember from the preceding chapter, it cannot succeed in being ethical and thus it cannot yield a complete system of ethics.

The ethic of self-devotion, on the other hand, could also not produce a complete ethic, because it was too narrow-minded to become universal; in other words, it was limited to the relation and dedication between man and man, instead of widening its compass so as to include all life under the sun.

Only when these two systems integrate into a new unit, interpenetrating each other in such a blending that the ethic of self-perfecting may stand with both feet on the solid ground of a real and concrete mysticism (rather than a fancied and abstract one) and the ethic of self-devotion will widen its circle so as to include all life as valuable, nay sacred—only then will a system of complete ethics become possible.

Now, Schweitzer's ethic of reverence for life shows its truth also by including in itself the different elements of ethics in their natural connection. Up till now no ethical system has been able to present in its parallelism and its interaction the aspiration for self-perfecting, in which man acts upon himself without external deeds, and the activist ethic. But the ethics of reverence for life accomplishes this, and indeed in a way as to transgress academic questions and to produce a true deepening of ethical insight.

Schweitzer says that the surmisings and the longings of all deep religiousness are contained in the ethics of reverence for life. Yet this religiousness does not construct for itself a complete philosophy, "but resigns itself to the necessity of leaving its cathedral unfinished. It finishes the chancel only, but in this chancel piety celebrates a living and never ceasing divine service."

To us Westerners it may seem strange that Schweitzer himself writes that the ethics of reverence for life are not dependent on a thought edifice yielding a satisfying conception of life—the reason being that it arises from an inner compulsion. It need not answer the question about the significance which the ethical man's work may have for the preservation, promotion, and enhancement of life in the total happenings within nature. It will not be misled by the reflection that its share in maintaining and completing life is hardly worth consideration in the face of the tremendous and unceasing destruction of life occurring every moment through natural forces. "Having the will-to-action, it can leave on one side all problems regarding the success of its work." The decisive importance for the world lies in the fact that in the ethically developed man a will-to-live has appeared which is filled with reverence for life and devotion to life.

In the face of the ghastly drama of the will-to-live divided against itself which we experience all over and all the time, the will-to-live within me has come to know about other wills-to-live. It is now filled with a yearning to arrive at unity with itself, thus becoming universal.

To his questions—why the will-to-live experiences itself in this fashion in me alone; why I am able to reflect on the totality of being; and what the goal is of this evolution in me—Schweitzer says there is no answer. "It remains a painful enigma for me that I must live with reverence for life in a world which is dominated by creative will which is also destructive will, and destructive will which is also creative."

This manifestation of the will-to-live in me, desirous to become one with other wills-to-live, Schweitzer calls the light that shines in the darkness. The ignorance in which the world is wrapped is non-existent for him who has been saved from the world. Reverence for life throws us into an unrest, not known to the world, but it also gives us a blessedness which the world cannot give.

As we help each other, as we save an insect from a puddle, life has devoted itself to life and the depreciation or self-disruption of life is ended. As we choose for our activity the removal of this self-disruption (Selbstentzweiung) of the will-to-live, we learn to know the one thing needful and can leave on one side the enigma of the universe and of our existence in it.

Since Schweitzer achieved his breakthrough to his complete ethics not by some passive revelation, as it were, but by very laborious plowing through the soils of Indian and Chinese and other metaphysical theories, it is quite enlightening to look at his explanations about non-European ethics, too.

He mentions, for instance, that the distinctive feature of Buddhist religion consists first of all in his rejection, equally with the material enjoyments, of the asceticism and self-torture practiced by Brahmans and the disciples of the Samkhya doctrine and Jainism. The Buddha preaches that the renunciation of the world consists in attaining the inner state of deliverance from things and not so much in achieving the utmost renunciation outwardly. "He whose spirit is really free from the world can concede his right to natural needs without becoming worldly." Buddha was quite convinced about this after having himself experienced that he did not attain to enlightenment when he tormented and mortified his body, but when he took food again and discontinued self-torture.

And yet the ethic of compassion, so emphatically preached by the Buddha, is incomplete, says Schweitzer. It is limited by negation of world-and-life and the Master does nowhere demand that because all life is suffering man should bring help to his fellow man and to every living being.

There is no doubt about the great insight of the noble-minded principle in the Oriental religions (Jainism, Buddhism, etc.) called ahimsa and commanding non-killing and non-harming of any life, since that doctrine considers all life as one and sacred. In this context we should mention this story, which Charles R. Joy brings in *The Animal World of Albert Schweitzer*:

A fatally tuberculous woman named Fan was ordered to eat the brains of a hundred sparrows as a remedy. But at the sight of the birds in the cage, she sighed and said, "Must it be that a hundred living creatures are to be killed that I may be healed? I would rather die than permit them to suffer." And she released them from the cage. Shortly thereafter she recovered from her disease.

Here we have an example of devotion to animal life at the risk of one's own life. We must conclude from it that such self-sacrifice is inherent and even active in those religions in spite of an intellectual compassion which does not demand the Brahmanist and the Buddhist to advance to the compassion of deed.

Schweitzer writes the only hope which they can give, without being inconsistent, is to afford to the individual a glance behind the veil by telling him that he must die to life and world in order to rise to the passionless state. Comparing the Oriental creed, to which nothing in the natural world is of interest and which urges a living in the world of pure spirituality, Schweitzer points to the Gospel of Jesus, which calls on man to become free from the world and from himself in order to work in the world as an instrument of God.

As to the principle of ahimsa (non-violence), Schweitzer contends that it should not be considered as something in itself but as the servant of compassion and subordinate to it. It must, therefore, come to terms with reality in a practical way. A true reverence for ethics requires us to recognize the difference within it.

Indian thought could not avoid the practical grappling with reality, says the doctor, if it were concerned with the totality of ethics and not merely with the ethic of non-activity.

But once again, just because it lays down the not-killing and the not-harming as dogma pure and simple, it succeeds in preserving safely through the centuries the great ethical thought bound up with it.

On the other hand, the religions which stress world- and life-negation (Brahmanism and Buddhism) show no interest in civilization. In contrast to them, the Judaism of the prophetic period as well as the religion of Zarathustra and the Chinese creeds include strong impulses to civilization in their ethical affirmation of the world and life.

As to the ethical legacy of Jesus, it is above all Paul who, by his forceful message of the ethical character of the faith in Christ, becomes the true disciple of Jesus. To him, to believe in Jesus Christ requires to stand under the absolute authority of the ethical, drawing its warmth from the flame of love. The critical theologian Schweitzer, although admitting that the redemption to be achieved through a merging into spirituality has something grand about it, adheres to the Christian longing of a union in God leading to a living ethical spirituality, resulting in activity in the power of God. Such a redemption from the world is to him the only one which can satisfy the longing of the heart. Thus, although being aware of the charm of the logical religion, we abide by Christianity with all its simplicity and all its antinomies. "It is indeed true and valuable, for it answers to the deepest stirrings of our inner will-to-live."

It goes without saying that these innermost stirrings of my will-to-live cannot stop at a self-contained life, no matter how honestly I aspire after self-perfection. They will, above and beyond that, be constantly sparked by the impulse to devote myself; to take part in perfecting our ideal of progress; to give meaning to our life right here on earth. "This is the basis of our striving for harmony with the spiritual element."

Why do we feel that urge to devotion? Schweitzer maintains that thought must strive to elucidate the nature of the ethical in itself. By doing so it arrives at defining ethics as devotion to life inspired by reverence for life. It makes no difference that the phrase reverence for life sounds perhaps too general and somewhat lifeless; it nevertheless will keep a tight grip on the man into whose mind it has entered. Sympathy, and love, and every kind of valuable enthusiasm, are contained in this postulate; and it works upon our souls with restless living force, throwing them into the unrest of a responsibility which never ceases to affect us. "Just as the screw which churns its way through the water drives the ship along, so does reverence for life drive the man."

Reverence for life compels me to struggle for freedom not only from the destinies of life, but also for freedom from myself. Not only towards outside circumstances, but also with regard to my personal attitude towards the world, I practice the highest self-maintenance. "Out of reverence for my own existence I place myself under the compulsion of veracity towards myself." Any action in defiance of my conviction would amount to a purchase at too high a price. To be untrue to myself would make me fear that I were to wound my will-to-live with a poisoned spear.

Schweitzer explains that in the struggle which we have to carry on against the evil in our mankind, we have to fall back upon the struggle with the veracity towards ourselves as the means by which we influence others. We quietly draw them into our efforts for the spiritual self-realization sprouting from reverence for our own life. "Power makes no noise. It is there, and it works. True ethics begin where the use of language ceases."

Schweitzer believes that the innermost element in the activist ethics, though it may appear as self-devotion, comes from the compulsion to sincerity towards oneself. Only when the ethics of being other than the world rises from this source will it flow purely. Thus the reverence for life applied to my own existence and the one which prompts my devotion to other life, interpenetrate each other.

Whereas the ordinary ethical systems engage in discussions of conflicting duties because they are lacking a basic principle of the moral, the ethic of reverence for life can calmly take its time to think out in all directions its own principle of the ethical. Being firmly established, it can settle its position in the face of these conflicts.

Ethics must come to terms with three adversaries. Thoughtlessness, egoistic self-assertion, and society. As to our thoughtlessness, we do easily overlook it, since no open conflict arises between it and our ethics. And yet, this adversary obstructs our ethics unnoticingly. When it comes to the conflict with egoism, we can freely move in a wide circle without collision. Because we can accomplish many a good thing without actually shouldering any sacrifice. And even if a bit of a man's life may suffer, it is as insignificant as "losing a hair or a flake of dead skin." Schweitzer argues that over wide stretches of conduct the inner liberaton or the being different from the world, the veracity towards oneself and even our self-devotion to other life, amounts only to giving attention to that relationship between ethics and our egoism. Yet we fall so much behind, because we don't keep up to it. There is no sufficient pressure of any inward compulsion to be ethical. "At all points the steam hisses out of the boiler that is not tightly closed." These losses of energy are really high in ordinary ethics, because they do not possess a basic principle of the moral to act upon thought. Thus they cannot tighten the lid of the boiler, says Schweitzer; they do, moreover, not even examine it. Reverence for life, however, being always present to thought, permeates unceasingly and in all directions our observations, reflections and decisions. We are as much transformed by it as the water which has been colored by a dye-stuff dropped into it. The man's struggle with thoughtlessness has begun and must always continue.

As to the position of reverence for life in the conflicts between an inner compulsion to self-sacrifice and the necessary upholding of the ego, Schweitzer writes the following: I am also subject to the division of my will-to-live against itself. My life conflicts in a thousand ways with that of others, and I, too, am faced with the necessity to injure or to destroy life. My steps kill or harm tiny creatures, I defend or maintain my existence by annihilating rodents, insects, bacteria, and I gain my food by destroying plants and animals. And even my happiness is built upon injury of my neighbor.

In order to uphold ethics in the midst of the gruesome self-division of my will-to-live, ordinary ethics seek compromises: they try to dictate the measure of life and happiness to be sacrificed by me as compared to the part which I may retain at the cost of my fellow men's life and happiness. These decisions result in experimental and relative ethics, says Schweitzer. "They offer as ethical what is in reality not ethical but a mixture of non-ethical necessity and ethics." This causes a huge confusion, leading to an ever increasing obstruction of the conception of ethics.

The ethics of reverence for life do not offer a relative ethic. To them only the preservation and promotion of life rank as good; and all destruction and injury of life they condemn as evil. Instead of keeping in store adjustments between ethics and necessity ready made for use, they will in each given instance and in ever original ways attempt to come to grips in man with reality. They cannot free me of all ethical conflicts, but compel me to decide for myself in each case to which extent I can remain ethical and how much I must yield to the necessity for destruction and injury of life, therewith incurring guilt.

We cannot make progress in ethics by receiving instructions from society about agreement between ethical and necessary, but only by coming to hear evermore distinctly the voice of the ethical, by sensing evermore the longing to maintain and promote life and by becoming evermore reluctant to destroy or injure life.

It is, as we remember, always the very subjective decision which must be arrived at in ethical conflicts. Our guiding star can only be the feeling for the highest possible responsibility towards other life.

We must never let ourselves become blunted. We are living

in truth, when we experience these conflicts more profoundly. The good conscience is an invention of the devil.

Schweitzer speaks of three things which are necessary for ethics. It must renounce all ethical interpretation of the world; it must become cosmic and mystical; in other words, it must conceive all the self-devotion in ethics as a manifestation of an inward, spiritual relation to the world; it must not fall into abstract thinking but must remain elemental self-devotion of human life to every form of living being.

The origin of ethics is that I think out the full meaning of the world-affirmation which, together with the life-affirmation in my will-to-live, is given by nature, and try to make it a reality.

The thinker in Schweitzer cannot resist protesting the point of departure in the philosophy of Descartes. "I think, therefore I exist." This paltry, arbitrarily chosen dogma irretrievably leads me on to the road of abstraction. It can never find the right approach to ethics and remains entangled in a dead world-view. True philosophy must depart from the most immediate and comprehensive fact of consciousness: "I am life which wills to live, in the midst of life which wills to live."

This is not an ingenious dogmatic formula. Day by day, hour by hour, I live and move in it. At every moment of reflection it stands fresh before me. There bursts forth from it again and again as from roots that can never dry up, a living world- and life-view which can deal with all the facts of Being. A mysticism of ethical union with Being grows out of it. (cf. Diagram 2)

Schweitzer asserts that everything which in the ordinary

REVERENCE for all LIFE

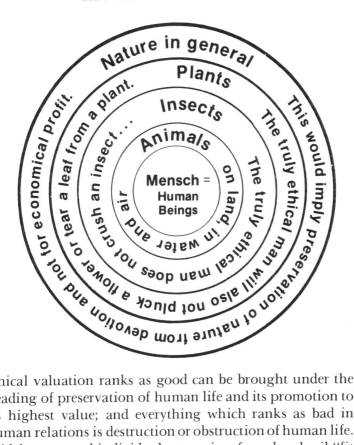

ethical valuation ranks as good can be brought under the heading of preservation of human life and its promotion to its highest value; and everything which ranks as bad in human relations is destruction or obstruction of human life. Widely separated individual categories of good and evil "fit together like the pieces of a jigsaw puzzle," once they are comprehended and deepened in the basic principle of reverence for life—this most universal definition of good and evil. The world-view of reverence for life takes the world with its horrors in the glorious and with the meaningless in the meaningful—as it is and as a riddle.

But that does not mean that we need stand before life at

our wits' end. The spiritual relation with the world which we gain through reverence for life is independent of all knowledge of the universe. "Through the dark valley of resignation it leads us by an inward necessity up to the shining heights of ethical world- and life-affirmation."

Why does Schweitzer put so much emphasis on resignation? It is to him the one possible way of giving meaning to our life—in that we raise our natural and passive relation to the world to a spiritual—by resignation. True resignation enables man, who feels his subordination to the world happenings, to win his way to inward freedom from the outward side of his existence. And it is the inward freedom which yields him strength to deal with all the hardships in his lot, thus making him a deeper and more inward person, purifying him, and keeping him calm and peaceful. "Resignation, therefore, is the spiritual and ethical affirmation of one's own existence. True world-affirmation can be won only by him who has gone through the stage of resignation."

By not living for himself alone, but feeling himself one with all life within his reach, man comes from an active relation to the world into a spiritual one.

Once a person has begun to think about the mystery of his life and the links connecting him with the life that fills the world he cannot avoid to subject his own as well as all other life to the principle of reverence for life and cannot resist to manifest this principle by ethical life-affirmation—expressed in action. His existence will thereby become harder in every respect, but it will also be richer, more beautiful, and happier. "It will become, instead of mere living, a real experience of life."

13. The Fellowship of Those Who Bear the Mark of Pain

"What we are, is nothing—what we seek, everything."

When Gautama* rose one night from his bed, abandoning his wife and child and royal glamour in exchange of a beggar's existence, he may have deeply felt the truth of these timeless words by Hölderlin.

So he set out into want and uncertainty and after the search for the cause of pain and sorrow. And the "truth of pain" manifesting itself in "birth, old age, sickness, death and sorrow" stands at the head of his Four Noble Truths.

And Gautama, "the Buddha," that is "the Enlightened," became, though not its founder, the foremost preacher of Ahimsa—and thus the creator of the ethics of compassion.

What Schweitzer writes about "The Fellowship of those who bear the Mark of Pain"** definitely approves of the Buddha's insights into the gruesome power of "the lord whose name is pain." The tropical doctor, who is pessimistic as to the purpose in the world-happenings, while his "willing and hoping are optimistic" gives a description of "Misery in Paradise" in such an impressive wording that

*563? to 483 B.C.
**The German "participial construction" lends itself well for that designation—"Die Gemeinde der vom Schmerz Gezeichneten"

77

it should be communicated to the reader: he saw a victim of sleeping sickness lying on the ground with his head almost buried in the sand and ants running all over him.

He was past all help, though he still breathed. While I was busied with him I could see through the door of the hut the bright blue waters of the bay in their frame of green woods, a scene of almost magic beauty, looking still more enchanting in the flood of golden light poured over it by the setting sun. To be shown in a single glance such a paradise and such helpless, hopeless misery, was overwhelming . . . but it was a symbol of the condition of Africa.

When Schweitzer made the unusual decision to begin the study of medicine at the age of thirty, some of his friends tried to persuade him that "the natives who live in the bosom of nature are never so ill as we are, and do not feel pain so much."

The doctor of Lambarene experienced that such statements were not true. Most of our European diseases prevailed there, he learned, and several of the hideous ones brought there by the white man produced, if possible, more misery than with us "and the child of nature feels them as we do, for to be human means to be subject to the power of that terrible lord whose name is Pain."

Above and beyond that misery, the primitive man is not only lacking our highly developed hospital facilities with pain relieving medications, but also the spiritual soothing of good literature, philosophy, great art and great religions.

The fact that a good deal of journalese has been spread by mediocre characters visiting Lambarene for a few hours or days, can never relieve us Westerners from those purely humanitarian duties which must not stop at national or racial borderlines—all the more as the Caucasian has incurred a heavy guilt towards the colonial peoples. We have no moral right to ignore Schweitzer's invitation to think what the last ten years of our family history would have been without medical help of any sort. "It is time that we should wake from slumber and face our responsibilities!"

Of course, there is a widely circulated slogan to keep us undisturbed and comfortable in our prosperity slumber: "Charity begins at home." But do those people who like to silence any charitable stirrings ever ask themselves from which motives our race subjected colored races to colonization and, moreover, dragged thousands of them out of their native surroundings—mostly by means and methods which were everything else but humane?

Because we are so fatally dominated by a purely economic mentality, many people consider medical help for the natives of importance only inasmuch as the "human material" should be preserved so that the colonies may not become valueless. Yet Schweitzer points with good reason to the fact which lies beyond economics, namely that we civilized peoples should not keep for ourselves alone the wealth of medical means to deliver men from sickness, pain, and death which science has given us. If we have retained any ethical thinking at all, the doctor argues, how can we refuse the benefit of new discoveries to those who, in distant lands, have to suffer even greater physical distress than we. Of course, governments send out medical men, yet they can fulfill only a fraction of the needs; therefore others must go out who are commissioned by human society as such. Whoever has personally learned what pain and anxiety are, must contribute to the transmission of help which came to him.

He belongs no more to himself alone; he has become the brother of all who suffer. On the "Brotherhood of those who bear the mark of pain" lies the duty of medical work, work for humanity's sake, in the colonies. Commissioned by their representatives, medical men must accomplish among the suffering in far-off lands, what is crying out for accomplishment in the name of true civilization.

And the "great doctor" states that it was the elementary truth embodied in the aid of the "brotherhood of those who bear the mark of pain" which made him venture to found the Forest Hospital at Lambarene.

To the question who the members of this fellowship are, our humanitarian answers: those who have experienced what bodily pain and anguish are, belong together the world over. It is a secret bond which unites them. Every one who has been delivered from pain must not think that he may continue his life as before, entirely forgetful of the past. His eyes have been opened as to pain and anguish and he must help in the battle against these two enemies. In poetical language (and certainly in memory of his fatal illness) the doctor urges those whose life has been saved from death or torturing pain, to contribute to the rendition of "the kindly anaesthetic and the helpful knife to begin their work, where death and torturing pain still rule unhindered." And the mother whose child still belongs to her—thanks to medical aid—"and not to the cold earth, must help, so that the poor mother who has never seen a doctor may be spared what she has been spared."

We had mentioned Schweitzer's pessimism—which, by the way, he has in common with all serious philosophers of culture—but we should also point to the fact that he never let himself get lost in brooding over the misery in the world; because he "always held firmly to the thought that each of us can do a little to bring some portion of it to an end." And he gradually found inner contentment in the knowledge that the only thing we can understand about the problem of universal misery is the fact that each of us has to go his own way, but with the intention to lend his help for deliverance.

It seems characteristic for most of us to minimize the burdens and hardships of men whom we consider to be geniuses. Yet, the opposite is true in most instances. And Schweitzer is a good example: he wrote that in his own life anxiety, trouble and sorrow had been allotted at times in such abundance that he would have broken down under the weight if his nerves had not been so strong. "Heavy is the burden of fatigue and responsibility which has lain upon me without a break for years." And he continues that he had not much of his life for himself, not even the hours which should be devoted to his wife and child.

This point is, by the way, one of those which shallow critics have held against him—namely that he did not live with his family in Switzerland. (His wife could bear the African climate for only short periods at a time.)

Another criticism runs like this: why did this veritable genius not devote all of his energies to the white race—instead of spending them for the benefit of the African Negroes.

There is no time nor space here to list all the weighty arguments for Schweitzer's universal deed and against critics, most of whom have either not read anything of his works or not grasped their philosophical value for life, humaneness and our world.

Back to the doctor's burdened existence: he mentions with gratitude also the blessings of being able to work in the service of mercy, and that with success; to have received "affection and kindness in abundance"; he mentions also loyal helpers; good health; a well-balanced temperament; and an energy linked with calmness and deliberation; and finally he speaks of whatever happiness fell to his lot.

It is characteristic of Schweitzer that all the pain and misery witnessed by him in his life could not make him lose courage and confidence. Quite on the contrary: the misery he had seen gave him strength, and faith in his fellow men supported his hope for the future; he expressed confidence that a sufficient number of people who have been saved from bodily suffering would respond to requests on behalf of persons in similar need. He also nourished hope that among physicians of the world there will be several ones to go out into various parts of the world in heeding the call of the fellowship of those who bear the mark of pain. In some place Schweitzer writes that Christianity, although it is, like all great religions, world- and life-negating by its creed, becomes nevertheless a constructive force due to the teachings and deeds of Jesus, to whom healing was as essential as preaching. In contrast to him and our basically active Christianity, the consistently world- and life-negating religions of the Far East and also Schopenhauer espouse a pity which is, in the last resort, not ethical but supra-ethical, not practical but merely theoretical, not devoted to active help and self-sacrifice but to an ideal of inactivity which obstructs the road to the real ethics of love.

The ethics of self-perfecting is also doomed to lip service and failure if the attainment of inward freedom from the world will not enable a person to work as a more direct force in the world. This thought is not present either in Schopenhauer nor in the Indians.

Schweitzer's ethics of reverence for life is very demanding, indeed. Its meaning and content urge the individual to action and sacrifice in all realms of life—be it in those of wealth or health, or in the intellectual and spiritual obligations to our fellow man and to society.

But the ethics of reverence for life are, with regard to possessions, "outspokenly individualistic"; that means that a person's wealth, whether acquired or inherited, should be used for the benefit of the community "through the absolutely free decision of the individual" and not by any measures of society. "Wealth must reach the community in the most varied ways, if it is to be of the greatest benefit to all."

With respect to health, the voice of reverence for life

summons us emphatically not to take our good health for granted and as a matter of merit, but to stretch out a helping hand to those who are under pain and strain and are in need of aid and comfort.

In this context, some of us may be reminded of the French philosopher Blaise Pascal, who, although suffering himself from bad health, took a much sicker person into his house in order to attend to him.

Schweitzer also speaks about the need for everyone of us to sacrifice some of our time, if not for a fellow man in physical pain, then perhaps for an old and helpless person, or somebody who suffers from loneliness, blindness or any other defect calling for assistance by a healthy individual who can spare a little time and energy for a brother or sister in distress.

The ethics of reverence for life also do not allow my rights to belong to me: I must not still my conscience with the reflection that I may use my greater efficiency at the cost of a less efficient man, regardless of how legitimate my means to advancement are. Reverence for life bids me think of others and ponder whether I can assume "the inward right to pluck all of the fruit that my hand can reach." By acting in such a way, namely in obedience to consideration of others, I may appear to the ordinary opinion as foolish. Moreover, if my renunciation proves to be of no use to him for whom I made it, it may even show itself as folly. "And yet I was right. Reverence for life is the highest court of appeal." Its commands carry their own significance in themselves, even if our action seems foolish or useless. We all look for the folly in the other person so that we may feel justified in our assumption that we carry higher responsibilities in our hearts. Yet it is only to the degree as we all become less rational [taken this word in the meaning of ordinary calculation] "that the ethical disposition develops in us, and allows problems to become soluble which have hitherto been insoluble."

Schweitzer writes that reverence for life will also not grant me my happiness as my own. In happy moments when I am about to enjoy myself without restraint, it stirs in me reflections about misery seen or suspected and it hinders me to drive away my uneasiness. I can never live my life for itself, just as the wave in the ocean cannot exist for itself. "It is an uncomfortable doctrine which the true ethics whisper into my ears." You are happy; therefore you should give much.

You must not accept as a matter of course, whatever you received more than others in health, working capacity, natural talents, success, harmonious childhood and family life. You must pay a price for them by showing more than average devotion to life.

The voice of true ethics is dangerous to the happy, if they listen to it. Its calls never damp down the irrational which glows within it. It assails them in order to pull them off their smooth track and make adventurers of self-devotion out of them, of whom the world has too few. "Reverence for life is an inexorable creditor!"

Yet, all those demands and claims which reverence for life advances into our faces and hearts, carry the blessings in themselves. They pull us out of our routine worlds which for many modern people are real industrial machine chores. Such persons and all the others harnessed into a daily monotony will experience genuine inward exaltations by working with men and for men.

So much about the relation and devotion between man and man. But how about our relation to all the non-human life? The reader has already gained some insight into Schweitzer's concern for all life, and his belief that all life is sacred. To the truly ethical man also that life which to us seems lower and less valuable is nevertheless sacred. And in all those decisions which he must make between two lives he must sacrifice, he is conscious of acting subjectively and arbitrarily, knowing that he is responsible for the life which he sacrifices.

Beginning with Saint Francis of Assisi European thought becomes aware that ethics must include the animal creation as well. And this new consciousness tells us that "ethics is reverence for *all* life."

In "My Word to Mankind," Schweitzer explains that the division of higher and lower, of more and less valuable life originated in man's purely subjective classification according to life which is more or less useful to him. Yet, who of us knows, asks Schweitzer, which value a given creature has in the cosmic plan? And "the absolute ethics of the will-to-live must reverence every form of life." The mystery of life is always too profound for us and its value is beyond our capacity of estimation.

We know that, in contrast to the great religions of the Far East, our Bible does not include compassion of man towards animals. And this may be one of the main reasons why there has been so much suffering inflicted upon animals in our Western societies. While the Jain monks—to give one example—go so far as to cover mouth and nose with a cloth so that they may not inhale the tiny creatures in the air, our civilized people have electrical devices plugged in, where the insects are dying by the hundreds on contact. To many Westerners the name "insect" alone suffices to stir the urge to kill. And the mass killing is organized and commercialized in well-functioning "pest" control companies.

It is interesting to find a parallel to Schweitzer's concern for the protection of insects from being burned by lamps in Lev Tolstoj's *War and Peace*, where we read of a man who tries to chase away the insects from a lighted lamp.

It is true that crops can be damaged or even destroyed by insects but extensive research has shown that many of these can be controlled through natural means. Australia experimented successfully in protecting their fruit trees by importing certain species of birds. Naturalists have also proven by empirical evidence that without insects even the most fertile landscape would turn into a desert. In summary, even in the area of agricultural pest control management, Schweitzer's principle of reverence for life can prove to be a workable guide in developing a more sound and sane ecology.

And what about the incessant suffering inflicted by men against horses and other domestic animals to whose toils and to whose meat we owe our existence? The tropical doctor laments about the superfluous pain to which testing animals are subjected in medical schools in order to illustrate to students reactions of the living body which are known to them without such tortures. In other instances, says Schweitzer, the animals are not given anesthetics so that a little time can be saved.

Above and beyond that there is constant torturing going on in laboratories for behavioral psychology. To give just one example of some of the most blood curdling (and yet not "out of the ordinary") experimental procedures, I think of a report in a U.S. magazine. The article tells of a person who was "told to torment and frustrate the monkeys and watch their reactions." And a professor is quoted to have stated: "There is no way to walk into that facility without feeling that you're in some kind of hell." We also read that some of the last seventeen monkeys, which had to be removed by the police, were "in such a state of physical and mental stress that they had bitten off their fingers and arms."

All these and other pains inflicted by men onto animals make us understand what the tropical doctor writes about the tremendous guilt of man towards not only the colonial peoples, but just as well to animals, birds, fish, insects, and other forms of life. When will the so-called Homo sapiens develop into a being to which Pascal's dictum will no longer apply: everyone wants to become king—but no one a human being.

14. What Can Be Done?

In his "Oration on the Dignity of Man," Pico della Mirandola (Giovanni) lets God speak thus to the son of Adam:

> I have set you in the midst of the world so that you may perceive so much easier what is in it. I have made you neither a heavenly nor an earthly, neither a mortal nor an immortal creature, so that you may chisel out your features as your own sculpture. You can degenerate to a beast; but you can also achieve a rebirth to a godlike being out of your spirit.

This excerpt from Egon Friedell's magnificent "Kulturgeschichte der Neuzeit" (*A Cultural History of Modern Times*) seems to lend itself quite well as an introduction to our final chapter, in which we ask the reader to join us—and to assist us*—in our wondering and pondering about what can be done to rescue our fatally disintegrating culture from its final decomposition or "decay," which by necessity of natural impact would entail the collapse of not only our

---

*Feel free to tell us (Doug Anderson or me) your ideas and/or criticisms.

Western civilization but also the closely linked cultures of the non-Western world. For we have become "one world"—but not in the spiritual jargon of the politicians, nay, much rather in the destiny-doomed rhetorics of cosmic forces—which will yield their fatal right-of-way to man's drive and control only to that extent which man deserves as long as he willingly and conscientiously chooses that branch of his road which leads him to the godlike image, personification, and realization and away from that dismal road, which millions of people consider as the "realistic" or even "reasonable" way of life; that one, the road of economic exploitation (not used here in the strictly Marxian sense), political usurpation, public sensations, and social deterioration.

It is high time, I believe, that we wake up from our sugar-coated-pill-taking of self-deception, this twin sister of wishful thinking, which makes us dance on the smooth and comfortable carpet floors of that "Titanic" which lulls us into an optimistic gilding of the setting sun—called modern civilization.

"But what can be done?" the reader will ask. And "Is there any solution?"

And I must admit that we have no straight answer in the sense of "yes" or a positive remedy, or "no" in a negative direction.

And still we can, if we consider and weigh all the positive or constructive traits of modern mankind, join in and confirm of Schweitzer's hope that manhood will not tread its road to the final ruin.

But what are these constructive features of our modern humanity?

Let all those who are aware of the precarious state of our world and life integrity try to think of the elements of world and life preservation and consider them as they come to mind, that is not classified according to imagined weight and importance.

There is inherent in all of us the inner drive to self-perfection. It shows itself especially eye-catching in the field of sports—so dangerously overemphasized because of our materialistic disposition.

It also becomes quite obvious in the performing arts—music and others; less evident in the purely intellectual and spiritual realms—but it definitely exists here, too.

These urges toward self-perception make us believe in their constructive momentum and that they will stimulate a regeneration of humanitarian aspirations and faculties.

There is, to be sure, idealism present and active in all men, and Schweitzer points to the fact that there is more idealism at work than we do generally expect. It may often hover in the air without a clear direction and content, but we hope that these requisites can be analyzed and bundled.

One of the best proofs for the existence of effective idealism is the fact that Schweitzer's medical achievements were made possible largely by the contributions of idealists from all over the world.

As to the Western man's inherent drive towards activity, Schweitzer frequently ascribes to it those accomplishments of civilization which the Western mind had produced. And isn't the doctor himself one of the most eloquent examples for this restless activity?

And yet, our sense of objectivity and justice forces us to admit that this quality is probably responsible for much of the vehemence and violence of our race. Therefore it is of paramount importance precisely as to this trait that content and direction must provide that balance of mind and soul without which the Western societies would be endangered to lose their humanity.

It was Goethe who emphasized that our lives must be dedicated to a "valuable activity." But we think that Schweitzer's basic principle of reverence for life does specify the call of the hour in the direction of the most urgent necessity.

If our contemporary computer-dominated society will not succeed in developing an effective world-view yielding content and orientation, it will keep stumbling from one world war into the other like a drunkard staggers from one ditch into the other. The activity of both organisms proceed in such circumstances under propulsion of mere instinctual and unbalanced emotions and by expulsion of balanced reason. Yet the day will come—we dare to predict—when our "most civilized" Western mankind will channel its deep-seated drive to activity into new and constructive outlets and away from any activity geared to nothing else but "bread and games," or sensations at any cost and mostly gauged by a degree of dehumanizing violence.

If the Westerner still nourishes hope to be not merely a colonial malefactor in our visited world, but a true benefactor and a helping leader to underdeveloped peoples, then he better wake up to the dreadful truth of the dictum: "Our most underdeveloped territory lies right under our scalps."

Yes, helping hands in our tottering world we must and can become. The fact that many individuals are spending time, strength and money in voluntary services (to the blind, the aged, weak or handicapped, to abused children, etc.) fosters our confidence in the positive results of so much active kindness.

As to my humble self, I can assert that the general kindness of the American public, particularly of the employees in business and civil service establishments, compares very favorably with the general kindness in European countries known to me.

We believe that all living beings, whether of human or non-human life, will experience much furtherance if some of the general activity will be directed—by letters or other forms of communication to persons with influence—towards the dissemination and implementation of Schweitzer's humanitarian legacy.

There is hope in the fact that the history of warfare offers at least some evidence towards humanization, perhaps only with the individual soldier whose behavior in and out of combat is more humane than that of the medieval mercenary. (There is hardly any case where a contemporary soldier would debase himself to the point of throwing an infant into the fire.)

Further, the creation of the Red Cross points into the direction of a more humanized warfare.

Of course, we must not deceive ourselves about the dreadful dehumanization effected by war as such. Moreover, the killing and injuring of men by men constitutes that suicidal disruption of the will-to-live, which causes mankind not only to annihilate its own species—in contrast to the animals' instinctive self-preservation—but to sink, moreover, beneath the animal in all those cases where man's primitive instincts are no longer controlled but rather unleashed and manipulated by his reason.

The incomprehensible and depressing fact that it is exactly the adherents of the religion of love who have been engaged in a multitude of wars, including the Thirty Years' War and the equally bestial World Wars, seems to confirm Schweitzer's contention about the deterioration of thinking as well as of spiritual sway over the souls of Christian peoples.

By this we do not imply that our Christian churches have not been working towards a cultivation of man's spirit, and we could list a number of positive facts:

The believers are exposed to religious teachings; many of them are being stimulated to ponder about phenoma which stand above material goods; others are induced to do good works by stretching out a charitable hand to the needy within and without their countries; many people find that inner comfort and shelter which the outside world cannot yield them.

On the other hand, we have to admit the tragic fact that Christianity in its present garb is no longer a spiritual force capable of preventing the Christian nations from strife and warfare. To meet the reader's potential question why Christianity was lacking the commandment of compassion with animals, and even with slaves, we answer with Schweitzer:

The explanation must be sought in the fact that primitive Christendom lived in the expectation of the speedy end of the world and therefore believed the date to be near when all creatures would be delivered from their sufferings. St. Paul speaks of the longing of the whole creation for early redemption in the eighth chapter (verses 18-24) of the Epistle to the Romans.

And yet we must and do cherish confidence that the cultural power of gravity will cause the pendulum of the irrational phenomena of inhumanity, violence, cruelty, and outright torture to swing back to those humane aspirations which the rationalists of the Enlightenment brought to the surface. As he dwells on the humanitarian blessings of the Enlightenment, Schweitzer also mentions the abolition of torture by Frederick the Great of Prussia (1740-1786). This "most humane king and most kingly human" (Thomas Carlyle?), whom the French, who had suffered defeat at his hands, named "the philosopher on the throne," acted as an individualistic outsider and against the prevalent jurisdiction. And now, more than two centuries "ahead," our legal systems tolerate not only police brutality but outright torture, thus coercing entire associations, for example "Amnesty International," to spend energy, time and money in combating torture. One must surmise that it will be precisely the Christian nations who will finally experience a reversal in mental disposition and will find their way to a world-view which will send its roots back to the reverence for life of Jesus and up into the unfolded branches of Albert Schweitzer's reverence for life.

We spoke of the power of reason or of our minds, and we hope that it will gradually achieve a real encompassing elevation of the Homo sapiens, that it will, in other words, effect that insight in man which will make him aware of all the constructive achievements to be gained in the realm of spiritual needs and blessings as soon as our material urges will be less emphasized and as soon as more people will embrace the ancient truth that man lives not by bread alone.

We like to nourish the confidence also in modern man's insight to find the golden avenue between creeds, dogmas, ideologies, economic bazaar barrages, etc., by falling back and relying upon the much neglected reality of the human soul (or "psyche"), the functions and importance of which finds ever more recognition not only among psychologists but also from the medical profession.

One of the most outstanding psychological authorities, Carl Gustav Jung, points to the fact that during the last few decades a serious interest in the mysterious workings of the psyche has arisen within a great number of persons whose inner problems can no longer be solved by clerical or by traditional medical care. And Jung put the finger on the right spot with this statement in his book *The Undiscovered Self:*

Virtually everything depends on the human soul and its functions. It should be worthy of all the attention we can give it, especially today, when everyone admits that the weal or woe of the future will be decided neither by the attacks of wild animals nor by natural catastrophes nor by the danger of world-wide epidemics but simply and solely by the psychic changes in man. It needs only an almost imperceptible disturbance of equilibrium in a few of our rulers' heads to plunge the world into blood, fire and radioactivity. (p. 97)

We dare hope that the Homo sapiens will gradually set all his ambition into the aspiration to live up more and more to this honorable designation, renouncing all those influences—both inward and outward by nature—which play skillfully on the huge organ of emotions, desires, wishful thinking, cravings, etc., and taking counsel only from his individual and independent thinking. We know, of course, that thinking can be of a double nature—namely purely intellectual speculation and calculation (Verstandesdenken) and soul-filled thinking (Herzensdenken). And it is this latter faculty which we trust will be more and more cultivated in our schools so that coming generations will find stance and balance within their own minds, and not in a questionable education which aims at the mere training of human beings in specialized fields to make them qualify for higher earning brackets at the earliest possible age. We believe that a well-rounded education and, to be sure, one which is founded and grounded in the ethics of reverence for life, will develop that mental and moral flexibility which will enable a person to stand his ground in more than just one trade.

This assumption is, besides, supported by an experience, which Schweitzer had as a prisoner of war in a French camp: some inmates complaining about the food were allowed by the commander to try doing a better job and they really did prepare better meals, though none of them was a cook.

So, we join in Schweitzer's confidence that where a man's work is motivated by love and devotion, he will be able to make up for the lack of training.

Since the arts constitute one of the most important facets of education, we hope that here, too, the pendulum will swing back and open the eyes of ever more people to the true values of constructive art. This hope of ours finds encouragement not only in professional writing, such as Henry Pleasants' *The Agony of Modern Music*, but also in the fact that the population at large has retained a feeling for true art. Pleasants mentions, for instance, that programs listing classical music are selling out the concert halls immediately; whereas those offering modern music leave the halls empty and so stays the cash register, which becomes the real yardstick for the public taste. But, in order to publicize the moderns, they are being "sandwiched between Beethoven and Brahms."

This is not to say that all modern music is poor, for many a modern composer, too, is able to write in the "traditional" style. We would like to call the attention of the music lover to music which can be called soul-filled in contrast to other forms which are lacking soul—perhaps often due to the fact that they voluntarily renounce rhythm, harmony and, most important, melody—which is the very soul of music; most of the time, however, many modern composers are lacking the faculty to create melody—so it seems to me.

Mediocre music may not yet become blunting or destructive to our souls. But our age, and only ours, has experienced a dehumanization to a degree that violent music has caused destruction of property and even injury to individuals, to an extent that motorized and mounted police have had to be summoned for the protection of both.

It is true that police were present also around concert halls some two centuries ago—but only for the prevention of hazardous overcrowding or fire.

We also take comfort in the fact that many young people spend much time and money on education in and for classical music, although many of them are aware that "there is no money in it." (This phrase, by the way, is one of the worst visiting cards of our society.)

The educational impact of the arts is so universal and so deep-reaching that we ask the readers to bear with us for a little while.

It was Dostojevskij who coined the phrase: "Beauty will redeem the world," and Solzenižyn elaborates on it in his Nobel Prize lecture.

Again, we dare hoping that here, too, the pendulum of culture will swing back and, by so doing, will bear these fruits:

That ever wider circles of music lovers will gain a deep insight into the great difference between music as "revelation" and as sensation. Beethoven, who clearly stressed the esoteric as "religious" essence of music, expressed once his experience thus: just as thousands of people who, getting married for the sake of love and making love their daily business, have never experienced the revelation of love, so have thousands of musicians who make music their daily business never experienced the revelation of music.

Indeed—only when we recognize the deep truth of Sidney Lanier's words that, as we listen to Beethoven, our hands involuntarily fold for prayer; and also realize a tendency of our hands to clench into fists at the exposure to violent modern music—only then do we get an inkling of the pernicious decline which has befallen much of our contemporary music. Clothed in a joke, one could say:

Beethoven wrote music inspired by the birds—the moderns write music just for the birds.

If Oswald Spengler was right in stating that music is the last contribution of the Western mind to the culture of the world (and Arnold Toynbee approved of it, I believe), then all the attempts of modern musicians to broadcast mediocre or computer-produced or even violent "music" become one more proof for *The Decline of the West*.

I'm afraid that many professional musicians, having also succumbed to the general crowd-thinking, do not realize to what extent music can be an elating, liberating and well-nigh healing spiritual force, or, at the other end, a debasing, intoxicating and well-nigh destructive power.

All profound minds had a distinct feeling for the timeless truth that esoteric beauty in great art is an ever ennobling and soul regenerating force. Therefore, we uphold our hope in a positive reversal within our educational systems to the effect that there will no longer be room for "students" who do not "drink at the fountain of knowledge, but just gargle" —or who will not grasp the warning of the chuckle, "Think small—great ideas upset everybody."

The visual arts of our present age compare to those of previous eras not more favorably than does modern music to the great forms of the "queen of arts." There is, indeed, a good deal of truth in Bertrand Russell's statement that the modern artist has only one alternative—either to be despicable or to be despised.

And yet, there is reason for hope in the fact that Lincoln's dictum (that some people can be fooled all the time, all people can be fooled some of the time—but that not all people can be fooled all of the time) is being quoted today more often than in previous decades. And it certainly applies with regard to many pieces of modern art. It is not uncommon at all that many of them elicit nothing but ridicule if not unprintable remarks. And it happens just as frequently that simple folks with an unadulterated common sense or feeling, when being presented with a modern "art work"—say, of wrecking yard fragments collected within a cyclone fence—and being asked about their opinion, will spontaneously come forth with: "Looks like a mess to me," or a similar remark.

In a booklet of musician anecdotes* we read that Igor

*Werner Hennig, *Zwischen Götterspeise und Ochsenmenuett*, Berlin, 1973, p. 114.

Stravinskij, when a custom's official one time inspected his luggage, did not succeed in persuading the officer that the suspected object was an invaluable portrait of himself by Pablo Picasso. He merely elicited the determined reply: "That is no portrait, that is the map of a fortress!"

Richard Strauss, whose art songs are veritable masterpieces, admonished one day the orchestra rehearsing his "Salome" with these words: "More courage, gentlemen! The more incorrect it sounds, the more it is correct."*

A string quartet by Gerhard Wohlgemuth was composed in a way that the instruments could hardly be coordinated with each other. And one time a member of the group reported that "On one tour we were so dislocated that we kept swimming to the last measure. At the conclusion a music critic stepped up to us and said: "I have heard this quartet several times but today it was the first time that I really understood it.'"*

As to our architecture, it can happen that a person, asking for the theater or an art building in a strange city, will be told, with a corresponding expression on the face: "Oh, just keep looking for the ugliest building in the city—that will be our most modern edifice."

We can, I believe, cherish quite a bit of confidence in that original wit and wisdom which dwells in many a simple person and which pops up spontaneously when some "smart aleck"—be he a politician, a salesman, an "intellectual," an "artist" or whatever—tries to pull a leg on the "simpleton."

Quite generally speaking, the spiritual danger in works of art found an expression in this statement by someone whose name I don't remember: the bad in art is really not the bad; for it is easily recognized as such. But the mediocre is the truly bad, because it is taken for the good.

*Zwischen Götterspeise und Ochsenmenuett

Our race has accomplished the inventions of gunpowder, of dynamite (and Nobel himself was horrified by it), machine guns, even nuclear weapons. Great technical inventions, indeed! Greatest, alas, in the threat of world-wide annihilation!

But let's not forget the achievement of printing! Yet the question forces itself upon our minds: did it turn out, in the last resort, as a constructive or rather a destructive invention? If we think, for example, that it is used to print music for our children to dance to—a "music" which, if played to a herd of apes, would probably chase them into deadly panics. And, after having recovered again, they would perhaps think: so this is Homo sapiens? Thanks to the heavens that we are only Homo apiens!

What about our mass media, especially the newspapers? Isn't it highest time that readers write to the editors and complain about "gunman's language": he pumped five bullets in a man's belly, or: he scattered the victims' brains all over the floor.

And yet this is not the worst in the "educational" effect. The worst is most impressively presented to our eyes—on television. Can we take any comfort in such chuckles as this: "Mother: I told you, TV is educational. Junior already knows how to spell homicide"?

"Oh, friends, not these sounds!" Let us intonate one more sound of hope: it is one of our faiths that eugenics, the science of improving the human race (and not only domestic animals and zoo prisoners) will elevate us human beings to a higher level and will, speaking with Meng-tse, widen the narrow gap between man and animal.

Speaking about animals, there is hope and confidence coming to our minds from the fact that there are organizations for the prevention of cruelty to animals. But we believe that the relation of man towards all non-human life needs a revision in the direction of Schweitzer's reverence for life;

moreover, the noble verse: "Never plague an animal in fun, for its pain and yours are one"* should be imbued in the hearts of all children not only from elementary school age on, but already in kindergarten, nay in the parents' home. Only in this way can we justify Schweitzer's belief that we Westerners—although we gladly admit that the Chinese and the Indians preached sympathy for animals before us and also laid down the ethical principles towards all creatures—with "what we are doing today . . . towards animals also has its significance" and can stimulate the Oriental ethics.

Since there is so much truly blood curdling torture of animals in our world, we must mention the great doctor's admonition, that those who experiment on animals in medicine to help mankind should never quiet their consciences because their cruel action may have a worthy purpose. In every single case they should ponder whether it is really necessary to subject an animal to this sacrifice. "And they must take anxious care that the pain be mitigated as far as possible."

> How many outrages are committed in scientific institutions through the failure to administer anaesthetics to save time and trouble! And how many others by subjecting animals to torture simply to demonstrate phenomena already generally known!

What Schweitzer says about animal torture finds horrifying confirmation in many laboratories, some of the bestialities reaching a degree to compel law enforcement authorities to intervene in order to save animals from lingering death in torture or even from self-mutilation by despair.

On my desk lies a magazine clipping showing a little

*Quale nie ein Tier zum Scherz, denn es fühlt wie du den Schmerz. (German saying) monkey's face, the sadness of which is truly heartbreaking; another monkey, fettered into a framework, immediately reminds one of the medieval torture devices displayed in museums.

In this connection we want to emphasize this paragraph from C. R. Joy's book, *The Animal World of Albert Schweitzer*:

> The ethic of reverence for life prompts us to keep each other alert to what troubles us and to speak and act dauntlessly together in discharging the responsibility that we feel. It keeps us watching together for opportunities to bring some sort of help to animals in recompense for the great misery that men inflict upon them, and thus for a moment we escape from the incomprehensible horror of existence.

After such atrocities it is a ray of light when we read about Schweitzer's experience in 1949 on United States soil, as reported by C. R. Joy. The great doctor was told about the airlift which brought food to the snowbound animals in the winter. He exclaimed, "Ah, what a magnificent feat! Vive l'Amerique!" And later, in Europe, he told Mr. Joy "he believed there was more reverence for life in America than anywhere else in the world."

In the face of our general dehumanization—and in spite of it—we muster all the inner strength and join Schweitzer in his confidence that our contemporary mankind will find the insight and the noble-heartedness to reach back and comply with the humane aspirations of the Enlightenment.

Although we are well aware of our era's "sophisticated" and faith disrupting mentality, we know that history has yielded more than one proof for the belief that "faith can move mountains"—perhaps the most persuasive confirmation being the personality of Jeanne d'Arc, the Virgin of

Orleans (1412-1431). It was the spiritual force of an unshakeable faith glowing in that humble peasant girl, who, being only seventeen years of age and lacking any formal education, had nothing to offer but her faith when she set out with the presumptuous claim to deliver France from the British invaders.

Each and every one of us who has not yet renounced soulfilled thinking (Herzensdenken) should lend his heart and hand for the rebirth of our visited mankind.

At the age of ninety years, Schweitzer (1875-1965) gave a summary of his noble legacy titled, "My Word to Mankind." In this address Schweitzer expresses his confidence that the force (not "violence," as one translation rendered "Gewalt" *) of the benevolent faculties of our soul constitute *that* force which will prevail over all violence. Let us close this book with a selection therefrom.

At the present time when violence, clothed in lie, dominates the world more cruelly than it ever has before, I still remain convinced that truth, love, peaceableness, meekness and kindness are *that* force which can still master all other forces of violence. The world will be theirs as soon as ever a sufficient number of men with purity of heart, with strength and perseverance, think and live out thoughts of love and truth, of meekness and peaceableness.

*Gewalt can mean violence, if the context implies this meaning. Otherwise the exact translation of violence is "Gewalttatigkeit" (of rape e.g. "Vergewaltigung"), while f.i. "Die Seelengewalt der Musik" is the Spiritual Force of Music; "Die Gewalt der Worte Jesu"—the force of the words of Jesus, etc.

References

For persons interested in pursuing the legacy of Albert Schweitzer, the following people and organizations may be contacted:

Douglas Anderson
624 Madera Ave., Apt. 28
Madera, CA 93637

Dr. Walter Ensslin
6620 Del Rey Avenue
Clovis, CA 93612

Marilyn J. Lohne
P.O. Box 10162
Fresno, CA 93745

Cindy Milne
12589 Morningside
Clovis, CA 93612

Michael L. Stumpf
4167 E. Alta
Fresno, CA 93702

Harald Suess
Rheinstrasse 4/11
A-4020 Linz/Donau
Austria

Lothar Van Stoeck
1524 E. Magill
Fresno, CA 93710

The above belong also to the ALBERT SCHWEITZER CIRCLE, a very informal fellowship without any obligations nor any catering to financial aid.

The Albert Schweitzer Center
Hurlburt Road — R.D. 1, Box 7
Gt. Barrington, MA 01230

The Albert Schweitzer Fellowship
866 United Nations Plaza
New York, NY 10017

President G. T. Smith
Chapmann College
Orange, CA 92666

Glossary

Bearing in mind how much truth there is in the Italian phrase, *Traduttore—traditore* (to translate is to betray), we must give our readers the benefit of the following explanations on German concepts—hoping that this will facilitate the precise understanding of Albert Schweitzer's liberating legacy.

Kulturphilosophie (history of civilization): In spite of my Ph.D. in history, I prefer the direct translation of the German *Kulturphilosophie* (philosophy of culture) and *Kulturphilosoph* (philosopher of culture) to our "history and historian of civilization"—mainly because the analysis and interpretation of mankind's culture appears to me more as a discipline of thought than of recording. It goes, of course, without saying that both fields require much emphasis on thinking. This preference does not, however, exclude an alternation between both terms in this book.

Weltanschauung: In the third edition of *Civilization and Ethics*, we find in the reviser's note that many writers, lacking an English word for the very encompassing meaning of Weltanschauung, simply use the German term—as, for example, the translator of C. G. Jung—and that Schweitzer himself defines *Weltanschauung* as the sum total of the thoughts which the community or the individual thinks about the nature and purpose of the universe and about the place and destiny of mankind within the world. From the various translations for *Weltanschauung* (theory of the universe, philosophy or conception of the universe, philosophy, or philosophy of life, outlook on life) we are selecting the direct translation, "world-view," used by C. T. Campion. As Mrs. L. M. Russell states, the one German word *Welt* does duty for the two English words, universe and world. Of course, the German will often use *Weltall, Universum,* or *Kosmos.*

Ethik: In her note on *Die Ethik,* Mrs. Russell states that this word, very simple in German, has induced some critics to question the use of the term "ethics" for anything but "the science of morality"; further, that one cannot speak of "an ethic." She mentions also that some writers are tempted to avoid this term because of the divergence of opinion in dictionaries as to the number of the word.

As to the various meanings of the term quoted by the reviser, we must refrain from repeating them, relying upon the reader's inquisitiveness applied to Schweitzer's and other authors' writings.

Yet the quotation of Bentham's definition of ethics as the art to produce "the greatest possible quantity of happiness" already here evokes the comments that the pursuit of happiness is definitely not the postulate and content of Schweitzer's "Ethics of Reverence for Life," and, moreover, that Friedrich Nietzsche rejected the British concept of ethics with the cynical remark: *Der Mensch strebt nicht nach Glück, nur der Engländer tut das.* (Man does not strive for happiness; only the Englishman does so.)

Spirit: the German word *Geist* is more encompassing than our "spirit." It can mean the spirit (of God), pure spirit, mind (mind and body), heart, soul, sense (in this sense), etc. As Mrs. Russell remarks, the German uses simply "spirit" and "spiritual" for our mind and spirit, mental and spiritual," and because of this wider meaning the translation may sometimes appear not quite appropriate. Besides, *geistlich*, spiritual, meaning clerical, takes the adjective ending *-lich*, whereas the philosophical or intellectual connotation ends in *-ig* (*geistig*). Just as a matter of interest, let us mention that there are more than five hundred word combinations with *Geist*.

Mysticism: Albert Schweitzer says that "we are always in the presence of mysticism when we find a human being looking upon the division between earthly and super-earthly, temporal and eternal, as transcended, and feeling himself, while still externally amid the earthly and temporal, to belong to the super-earthly and eternal." Webster defines it as being "any doctrine that asserts the possibility of knowledge of spiritual truths through intuition acquired by fixed meditation."

Schweitzer further elaborates by writing, "And if in the last resort the aim of a world-view is our spiritual unity with infinite Being, then the perfect world-view is of necessity mysticism. It is in mysticism that man realizes spiritual union with infinite Being."